"We need your prayers at this time.
We also need your financial support for
the vast ministry of evangelism that God
has entrusted to us. By films,
by the printed page, by crusades, by radio,
by television, we are seeking to get the gospel
to millions of people throughout the world
at this critical period of history.
We need your help. I'm going to ask you
to write a letter to me today—Billy Graham;
Minneapolis, Minnesota, that's all
the address you need. And now,
until this same time next week, goodbye—
and may the Lord bless you real good!"

—"HOUR OF DECISION"
RADIO BROADCAST, SEPT. 24, 1967

Dedication to

Arline, Joseph, Diane, Nancy, and Peter

MAZONSON

"God Bless You Real Good"

God Bless You Real Good

My Crusade with Billy Graham

BY ALAN LEVY

An Essandess Special Edition

New York

Billy Graham bites his nails. He licks his lips before
greeting you. Rising to address an audience, he invariably
puts both hands to his still wavy, still blond hair—as if to
straighten it or perhaps check that it's there. Like all other
public speakers, he is bedeviled by his own silver tongue: he
once commended the traffic-safety record of Memphis for
"150 days without a *fertility*" and, one awful night, the
phrase "hail fellow well met" came out as "hell wet male
fellow." then "male het well fella," then "whale het male
fella," and finally as "shucks, you folks know what I'm
trying to say." Just turned 50, he has to watch his blood
pressure and needs eyeglasses for reading. Anywhere in the

world, when he checks out of a hotel, he leaves behind a wastebasket full of belongings he meant to take with him. He likes to sleep until 10 or 11 when he can, which isn't often, and describes himself to friends as a "late mover." He is, in a word, human.

He is also, I discovered one Spring, *something* of an intellectual—and before this candid report on the very model of a modern mass evangelist is complete, you and I will stumble across Billy Graham on a Nietzsche jag and hear him condemn an Ingmar Bergman movie with ivory-tower detachment.

It was strictly in quest of the human side of Billy Graham, however, that I took a working vacation in Puerto Rico. There, he was conducting a nine-day crusade—one night in Ponce followed by eight days and nights in San Juan, concluding with an Easter sunrise service. Until the Spring of 1967, the human side of "God's special messenger to today's world" (as his Billy Graham Evangelistic Association "Teammates" proclaim him) had eluded me. I had seldom perceived the man behind the message in his four books that have sold more than three million copies in 32 languages; in the 38 books and millions of words that have been written *about* him; in newsreels and in thousands of still photos, almost always a trifle stiff; in his Sunday-night saturation of radio and his twice-a-year weeklong blanketings of TV; and even in a couple of half-hour personal interviews when I was a newspaper reporter.

The most striking evidence I'd seen of Billy Graham's humanity was in various shots of him conversing with young people (where the animation was theirs as well as his) and in one remarkable photo of Graham and his wife Ruth bathing in the waters of Jamaica. They are crouching in the Caribbean and obviously posing for the photographer. But, peering closely and gazing beneath the surface, I caught a wavy glimpse of them holding hands underwater. It was in the hope of more of same, better of same, and a wider variety of same that, late last winter, I booked passage for Puerto Rico.

My family and I arrived in Ponce three days ahead of Graham. Later, in San Juan, we stayed at the same Holiday Inn where he and his 25-man Team were billeted. (His wife, Ruth, had stayed at home.) In Puerto Rico, I was afforded leisurely access to a dozen of the key backstage figures in the Billy Graham success story . . . invitations to visit strategic Billy Graham Evangelistic outposts in Minneapolis, Atlanta, and London as well as the Graham home in North Carolina (all of which I did later) . . . a daylong interview with Graham himself . . . and innumerable possibilities of chance encounters, which, when necessary, could be easily prearranged.

For instance, learning that he was addicted to two-or-three mile trots along the water (I never saw him get more than his feet wet in Puerto Rico), I would station myself on our hotel beachfront and play in the shallow surf with my daughters, ages 2 and 3. Billy Graham never failed to stop and chat—and so I always went to the beach armed with suntan lotion and a couple of questions. More often than not, I was the one who would subtly discourage conversation after ten or fifteen minutes—in order to dump my daughters into my wife's lap, race back to the room, and jot down everything I could remember him saying.

One morning, the San Juan *Star* noted that the full moon was due and I recalled a member of the Graham Team remarking that "on nights of the full moon, Billy braces himself for trouble. We all do." Thus, as soon as Graham had greeted my family, I asked him: "What happens on nights of the full moon?"

With a grin—he has a boyish grin and a public smile—he promptly ticked off four moonlit nights to remember:

. . . In Indianapolis, as Billy Graham's converts or, as his organization prefers to call them, "inquirers" assembled beneath his rostrum, a woman in a brilliant green dress stood up and let loose a blood-curdling, spine-chilling scream that immobilized Billy Graham and turned every eye in the audience away from him. She gave six more screams, by which time an official was at her side trying to put a gag in her mouth. Before he could do so, the woman fell in a

7

"To lick hypertension . . . I choose the exercise route."

dead faint. When she came to, she identified herself as a respectable, articulate society matron with no history of past disturbance and no recollection of what she had just done.

. . . In Houston, a woman told her pastor that her husband had set out with a gun to "get Billy Graham," who was preaching in Dallas. He was intercepted in Fort Worth.

. . . In Los Angeles, a lady lunged at Billy Graham with a knife when he descended from the platform.

. . . And at full moon during the memorable 1957 Crusade in Madison Square Garden, one of the ushers (an elderly gentleman recommended by his church) planted himself in the center aisle. Armed with books and scholarly references, he waited until Billy Graham stood up to speak and then began to bellow a speech of his own. The man's inattention to his ushering duties, however, had already alerted Graham's boyhood friend and alter-ego, associate evangelist Grady Wilson. Two husky men pinned the usher's arms behind him while Grady Wilson covered his mouth before hustling him to the exit.

Billy Graham is well aware that the word *lunacy* originally denoted intermittent insanity dependent upon changes in the moon. "I talked with a scientist at Princeton who's working on the moon and human behavior," Graham told me that morning on the beach. "He said there definitely *is* a relation and that he would never, never sleep outdoors in moonlight. It disrupts the mind."

Cliff Barrows, Graham's songleader, was along for the jog and he chimed in: "The booker for Madison Square Garden told me he tries not to book events for full-moon nights. That's when the riots happen."

"I don't know if this applies," Graham went on, "because it happened during the day, but there was a full moon that night. I came home to North Carolina after a long trip and the police were there. They told me there was a man camped out in the woods who'd been waiting to 'get Graham.' They hadn't been able to catch him, but they were pretty sure he wasn't armed. So I went into the woods calling for him and he came to me. He was a recently discharged mental patient from Illinois. He said his relationship with his sister had deteriorated because of my preaching's influence on her. I talked with him a while and told him what I was about. Then I gave him fifty dollars, found a hotel room for him, told him how to get home by bus the next day, and phoned his family to tell them when to expect him."

A small crowd of bathers and a coconut vendor had congregated a respectful distance from us. Billy Graham acted as though he didn't hear the shrill Puerto Rican cry of "Beelygram!" that was punctuating our conversation. He rambled on about his home in Montreat, North Carolina, and how he'd had to move from the valley at the foot of Piney Ridge Mountain to the very top because of cranks, curiosity-seekers, and pilgrims:

"The Trailways buses used to stop down there and let out whole busloads of travelers just to sightsee. Now that we're on top of the mountain, our privacy is much better—but still not perfectly safe. One day, a well-dressed man drove up in a brand-new Chrysler and my wife went out to see what he wanted. He said he was the Messiah and he had a message for Billy Graham. Well, Ruth said I was in my study and couldn't be disturbed. The man got a little belligerent and shoved past her, but couldn't get the front door open. He started to tug at it and Ruth said to him: 'If you were really the Messiah, you'd be able to walk right through that door, wouldn't you?'

"This gave him a pause and he stepped back and began to think about it. After a couple of minutes, without saying a word, he drove down the mountain and—I was told later—parked by the lake. He took off his wristwatch and threw it into the water. He took $25,000 out of the glove compartment and threw *it* into the water. Then he released the car's emergency brake and let *it* glide into the water and sink.

"Somebody who'd been watching him called the police. They took him into custody. He was a prominent South Carolina attorney who had come unhinged all of a sudden. But I don't remember if there was a full moon around." *

My one innocent question having unleashed such a revealing flood of anecdote, I was reluctant to ask another before scribbling all this in my notes. Graham paused and, when I didn't fill the lull, he said goodbye, shook hands with several onlookers who stepped forward to introduce themselves, signed a couple of autographs, and started down the beach with a brisk stride that turned into a lope and then a steady jog.

---

* —"Graham has his share of visits from cranks and mental cases. Once when he was alone in the house except for [his son] Ned, the study door burst open and a young man with a wild look dashed in shouting, 'I've come to get you!' Before the fellow could land the blow Billy knocked him down, took him outside, held him on the ground and said 'Now what's your trouble?' The young man began to cry. At that moment an older man appeared and said the intruder was his son, who was crazy and determined to kill Billy, and that he had tried to stop him . . . Billy prayed with them both as he held the boy, who was taken away quieted." —from *Billy Graham: The Authorized Biography*, by John Pollock (1966).

"Running," Billy Graham told me on another occasion, "is my major form of exercise nowadays. Since I got down here, I've been doing the mile in eight-and-a-half minutes. You can tell the world that I've finally broken the nine-minute mile.

"A while ago, I was preaching in Boston and I sort of blacked out one evening. I went to a specialist, but I knew what it was even before I saw him—high blood pressure. Hypertension seems to affect the males in my family around age 45 as far back as anyone can remember. With my father, it didn't come until he was 52.

"The doctor said there were two directions I could take: the drug route or the exercise route. I chose the exercise and went to see some doctors at the University of Illinois who specialize in exercise treatment. They gave me about 60 tests—chinning, jumping, everything—to find out how bad off I was physically. The only test I did well on was reflexes. They said I had better reflexes than any of the Chicago Cubs."

Graham, who stands six-feet-2 and weighs between 175 and 184, drills himself like an athlete. Unable to go out for a run in a congested, celebrity-conscious city like New York or London, he will instead do a mile in his hotel room—100 yards running and then 100 yards walking, etc.

"The first time I went running," he recalled in Puerto Rico, "I thought I was going to die. Now when I come back from a two-mile run, it's like I've had a couple of hours' sleep. The doctors want me to breathe heavy. It cleans out my lungs and enlarges their capacity. They tell me to run till I'm exhausted. Anyway, I have to keep running for a couple of weeks more. *Parade* Magazine's going to show me running on its cover and everyone's using me as an example of running for physical fitness."

At Hiram Bithorn Stadium in San Juan (named after a former Cub and White Sox pitcher who was the first Puerto Rican to play in both major leagues), the local Crusade organization had built Billy Graham a little white shack in which to meditate. Here, both before and after each sermon, a young doctor took Billy Graham's blood pressure "so I can tell the Mayo Clinic how I'm doing." One night, the doctor arrived late and hurriedly applied his paraphernalia to Graham's arm. His reading was alarmingly high.

"You cannot preach tonight," said the doctor.

"You do it over, son," said Billy Graham, "and this time do it carefully. I want to preach tonight and go running tomorrow."

This time, he passed.

I asked Billy Graham if he had given up golf for running.

"No," he said. "The doctors don't really like golf as an exercise for me, but I do. I like the company of golfers. And I like the way it takes up your mind; on the golf course, I'm thinking only about golf.

"Richard Nixon said something to me a year or so ago in New York. He said he had quit golfing. It takes up too much time, he said. 'I only have 15 more years in the prime of life,' he said. There are too many books to read, he told me. There are too many things to do. He wanted to know if I realized how much of a man's life he spends on the golf course.

"And I said to Mr. Nixon: 'Wait a minute. *I'm* the preacher and here *you* are preaching to *me*."

William Franklin Graham is THE preacher for our times. In *Modern Revivalism*—a study of famous American evangelists including Charles Grandison Finney, Dwight L. Moody, Billy Sunday *, and Billy Graham—Professor William G. McLoughlin, Jr., concludes that

> Finney's emphasis on God's moral law, Moody's on the atoning blood of a burden-bearing Christ, Sunday's on muscular Christianity, and Graham's on the need for repentance, all suited the particular spirit of their times. And in the same way their personalities suited their times: Finney, the argumentative frontier lawyer;

---

* Billy Sunday, the reformed ballplayer who sometimes started his service by running across the platform and sliding up to the pulpit, is probably the first evangelist to whom Billy Graham was exposed. At the age of 4, Graham was taken to hear Sunday in Charlotte, N. C. He has scarcely any first-hand recollection of the experience, other than being "held silent by the warning that if I squirmed, Billy Sunday would personally run me out of his tabernacle."

Moody, the aggressive, enterprising drummer; Sunday, the slangy sport, and Graham, the cleancut college boy. . . .

Insisting that each sought "to harness God's magnetic power to human ends," McLoughlin goes on to lambaste them all for having "compromised with American secularism on its own terms," having "done more to make men conform than to reform," and having "no fresh insights to offer to meet . . . the problems of their age." He accuses Graham and his Team of practicing the "engineering of mass consent" and he attributes their phenomenal success to the public desire for simplicity and certainty in an increasingly complex world.

To detractors like McLoughlin, Graham wisely turns the other cheek and points out that no man is wise enough to evaluate an evangelist's work until many generations have passed: "What good my ministry has done, I'll never know until I get to heaven. Then I may find that some obscure preacher working in a slum mission somewhere has done more to advance the kingdom of God than I have."

No such eternal judgments will be made here. This is simply an impressionistic portrait of Billy Graham—a man in motion—caught *the way he is now:* vibrantly alive and alert; all his senses finely tuned to every nuance of his silent audience, every change in his environment, every stress and strain in the magical chain that links man to God. This "man with God's message for these crisis days" (as he is introduced on the radio each Sunday night) is not easy to pin down on the printed page. To transmit the full-bodied fervor of a modern mass evangelist, the medium must be the message—in this case, a sermon that Billy Graham delivers a dozen times a year, but has yet to *plow* through once.

> *"Tonight my topic will be 'The Wickedest Man Who Ever Lived.' In Chicago, when I announced one night that this would be my next topic, a lady sent me a Special Delivery letter: 'I know the wickedest man alive. He's my husband.' And she listed 29 sins of his. Now you may*

"If I want realism, I read the first chapter of Romans."

think of someone you know. Or you may think of Hitler.
Or you may think of Mao Tse-Tung and all the people
whose lives he made miserable. Who do you think it is?
Hitler? Mussolini? Eichmann? Soon you'll find out."

It is in the ebbs and flows of public meetings that we truly
experience Billy Graham. These are usually held on neutral
secular ground such as a ball park, sports arena, race track,
dog track, State Fairground, exhibition hall, or armory.
Weather permitting, an outdoor site is preferable, for the
Billy Graham Team has found that non-churchgoers will
come more readily to an open-air Crusade. The meeting lasts
90 minutes and much of the crowd is still drifting in during
the first half—before Billy Graham stands up to speak.
Those who come early are rarely bored. On opening day in
San Juan, there was a parade featuring flags of 100 nations
borne by girls in white gowns, a majorette strutting in stars-
and-stripes, and for "Beelygram" heemself, a snappy
eleven-man motorcycle escort called the Road Runners. But,
any time and anywhere there is a Billy Graham meeting,
there is good cheer, good prayer, and, in particular, good
music.

> O Lord my God! When I in awesome wonder
> Consider all the worlds Thy hands have made,
> I see the stars, I hear the rolling thunder,
> Thy pow'r throughout the universe displayed.
>
> Then sings my soul, my Saviour God to Thee;
> How great Thou art, how great Thou art!
> Then sings my soul, my Saviour God to Thee;
> How great Thou art, how great Thou art! *

Sung in any of a dozen different tongues, this opening
anthem is a work of sweet, compelling grandeur—and, like
almost everything connected with Billy Graham, a story
goes with it. During the 1954 London Crusade, which at-
tracted more than two-million attendance in three months,

George Beverly Shea, who sings gospel for the Graham Team, was accosted on Oxford Street by an elderly Scotsman. "I've coom across a hymn aye think y'ought to see," said the old man, handing over a sheet of what Shea calls "Russian hieroglyphics." The song—originally written in 1885 by a 25-year-old Swedish pastor named Carl Boberg—had spread to Germany in 1907 and Russia in 1927. An English missionary, the Rev. Stuart K. Hine, came across it in the Ukraine, where he and his wife sang it as a duet at revival meetings. "Some time later," says the blurb from its publisher, Manna Music of Hollywood, "in the inspiring mountain scenery of Sub-Carpathian Russia, Mr. Hine was moved to translate the first three verses from Russian to English. After Mr. Hine's return to England, he sang the three verses at Gospel meetings during World War II, and added the fourth verse in 1948." Hine's translation accompanied the manuscript the Scotsman handed to Bev Shea.

"I want you all still. Tonight may change your life."

George Beverly Shea's is last voice before Graham's.

With a couple of alterations to suit the singer (*Mighty Thunder* became Rolling Thunder and "all the *works* Thy hands have made" became *Worlds*), *How Great Thou Art* not only ranks as Shea's most requested song, but also has been recorded by Kate Smith and Elvis Presley. In the 1957 Billy Graham Crusade at Madison Square Garden, it was sung 99 times in 97 nights.

"The reason I like *How Great Thou Art*," Billy Graham has said, "is because it turns Christians' eyes toward God rather than upon themselves. I urge Bev Shea and Cliff Barrows to use it as often as possible because it is such a God-honoring song."

George Beverly Shea, 59, "America's Beloved Gospel Singer" won the 1965 "Grammy" award as the nation's "finest singer of sacred and religious music." He is a granite-faced Canadian with a resounding baritone voice. From the outset, that voice has been one of the sublime treasures of the Billy Graham Evangelistic Association. Shea's is a deep-down baritone and, particularly when he sings *He's Got the Whole World in His Hands,* he reminds one of a W.A.S.P. Mahalia Jackson.

The son of a Wesleyan Methodist minister in Ottawa, Shea was working in 1943 as a radio announcer for WMBI in Chicago, where he also played the organ and sang hymns every morning at 8:15. One day, the bright-eyed young pastor of a basement church in suburban Western Springs, Illinois, barged past a receptionist who said Shea was too busy to see anybody. Shea's caller had just taken over "Songs in the Night," a popular Sunday-night program of music and meditation on WFCL. He had decided to revitalize the music. Bev Shea has never been able to say no to Billy Graham and they went on the air together early in 1944.

Describing the wartime-model Billy Graham,* Bev Shea told me:

"From the moment you laid eyes on him, you knew he was someone who'd be heard from again in the ministry. He had enthusiasm and ready wit and he was all he-man.

"My wife and I had an apartment in Chicago and she was ill with pernicious anemia. After I'd known him a few weeks, Billy said, 'You need to move out to Western Springs. I have just the place for you.' I said, 'I don't have the money' and he said, 'Well, Ruth and I are renting too.' I move slowly and, having just moved *to* Chicago, I wasn't ready to move *from* Chicago. But one Saturday, we drove out to look at the place he had in mind for me. To this day, I

---

* In October, 1944, Billy Graham was commissioned a second lieutenant in the U.S. Army Chaplain Corps with orders to await a training program at Harvard Divinity School. Before he could begin his training, however, he was bedded down for six weeks with a particularly virulent and painful case of mumps. As a convalescent, Billy Graham would have spent his military hitch behind a desk. As an ordained minister, however, he was able to resign his commission and turn his full time to evangelism.

can still remember that when we got there, the first thing we saw was Billy and Ruth standing in the timothy hay with Billy jumping up and down saying, 'This is your house, Bev! This is the one you take!' It was a little square brick thing and the asking price was $8,900. We made a down payment of $500. . . ''

As a onetime parishioner, Shea afforded me a glimpse of Billy Graham "in a little church situation like the one we had in Western Springs. Bill exuded cleanliness and sincerity, no ballyhoo. He liked to tell us he was a farm boy and joke about himself. People were captivated. He wasn't as conservative in his presentation as he is now. He'd leave the pulpit and stray three or four feet across the platform just to make his point.''

Young pastors are seldom paid a living wage. Sometimes something more than sincerity could be perceived shining through the gabardine suit he wore every day. "There were some rich men in the church,'' Bev Shea recalls, "and one day one of the deacons offered Billy $50 to buy a new suit. Billy told me how much he was tempted: 'I like that man. But suppose an argument came up in which I favored him or didn't favor him. So I diplomatically declined.' And this man was so impressed by Billy's ethics that he became one of his closest, most trusted advisors.''

Bev Shea, too, remained on call. Later in 1944, a network radio career opened up for him on ABC's "Club Time,'' where he served as a soloist until 1952. "There were no jets then and the networks wouldn't rely on tape,'' said Shea, wincing at hardships past, "and so I used to fly from wherever Billy was crusading to Chicago for the broadcasts. I remember, when we were in Los Angeles in 1949, that it cost me $264 round-trip just to fly in to do a 15-minute program.''

That Los Angeles Crusade in the "Canvas Cathedral''— a tent pitched in a vacant lot on the fringe of downtown— was the making of Billy Graham as an evangelist. His conversions of several lesser luminaries triggered local publicity, drawing such crowds that the Crusade was extended from three weeks to eight. This allowed time for national

Songleader Cliff Barrows really lives on Melody Lane.

recognition in *Time, Life* and *Newsweek*. And Bev Shea benefited from the exposure, too. In 1950, RCA Victor signed him to a recording contract and has released 27 of his albums so far.

"Every now and then," Shea told me, "Billy kids me about 'Whatever became of that little house I found for you in Western Springs?' Erma and I still live there, but now we've just added and added onto it until now it's a big long ranch house. We're 23 minutes from O'Hare Airport and I boast that, no matter where we come from, I'm the first member of the Team to get home."

At a Billy Graham meeting, more of the good music and much of the good cheer come from Cliff Barrows, who is as much cheerleader as song leader. Barrows, who tried to tell me that "they need me on the Team like a fifth wheel" knows better than that. In fact, when Billy Graham was asked publicly in 1965 what would happen if he died or retired from evangelism, he replied: "We've discussed this. It is generally understood that Leighton Ford [an associate evangelist who is married to Billy Graham's sister Jean] or Cliff Barrows would take my place. Cliff is a fellow with tremendous stamina and temperament. If you asked me who was the greatest Christian I know, it would be a toss-up between Cliff and my wife."

Barrows, 45, co-heir apparent *, is an ordained Baptist minister who looks like a photostat of Billy Graham. Dark, hairy, and handsome, he *appears* to be fiery and smoldering —until he speaks in a voice that is smooth and genial, even bland:

"Many people have come to the service tonight and we welcome you indeed and we hope the service is a very special blessing for you. And here is a very special announcement. Part of this meeting is being recorded for the 'Hour of Decision.' We are going to share part of tonight's wonderful program with the 900 radio stations around the world that broadcast the 'Hour of Decision' each Sunday. Thousands of people have been praying for these meetings . . . Now George Beverly Shea and the others are going to sing for you in just a few minutes, but first we'd like *you* to sing for *us*."

The selection for tonight is number 9 in the Billy Graham Crusade songbook (50 cents), *Stand Up, Stand Up for Jesus*. In order to conduct both the audience before him and the 200-to-2,000-voice locally-recruited choir behind him, Barrows waves his arms and spins like a whirling dervish. After the first stanza, he leans into the microphone to say: "It sounds good from up here. And, if you haven't joined

---

* Any discussion of a possible successor to Billy Graham must be tempered by history. An evangelistic organization rarely, if ever, outlives its evangelist by very long.

in, I think you've missed out on a very special blessing."
The volume swells and, after the next stanza, he says:
"Let's do the first stanza one more time for those of you
who didn't know it before."

Cliff Barrows met Billy Graham just after V-E Day when
Barrows was assistant pastor of Temple Baptist Church in
St. Paul. On June 7, 1945, he had married Billie Newell, a
United Brethren minister's daughter from Freeport, Illinois, and they honeymooned in Asheville, N.C., 15 miles
from Black Mountain, where a Youth for Christ rally was
under way.

(Youth for Christ was an evangelistic organization that
had begun in Chicago and Minneapolis a year earlier to provide a clean, exciting, uncompromisingly Christian alterna-
tive for servicemen who came to town on Saturday night.
It had spread like a brush fire to smaller cities and continued to illuminate Protestantism well into the 1950's, by
which time the average church was no longer dark on
Saturday nights.)

That Saturday night the speaker was the fiery young
evangelist from up Chicago way. The Barrowses had heard
a lot about Billy Graham (and Cliff had heard him preach
a year earlier at a Youth for Christ rally in Minneapolis).
They went to listen to him, but, when the regular song
leader failed to show up, the honeymooners were "drafted."
Cliff led the singing, Billie played the piano, and Cliff remembers now that Billy Graham's first observation was:
"We don't have much choice now. We're about to begin."

Billy Graham preached that night from Paul's letter to
Timothy ("Retreat, Hold the Line, Advance") and Cliff
says, characteristically, that "we all had a real good time."
Thus was formed—on an informal, part-time basis—the
Billy Graham Evangelistic Team, with Billie Barrows as
pianist sometimes singing duets with Cliff, who also played
the trombone. A year later, Billy Graham—as first vice-
president of Youth for Christ International—was invited to
preach in England and he invited the Barrowses to ac-
company him.

"We had a tremendous time in England," says Cliff

Barrows. "That was where I felt that God had called Bill and me to work together. I had thought I should try to preach, but now I found myself dedicated to the musical end of it and I've had peace of mind ever since." His wife stayed with the Team for five years and the Barrowses traveled everywhere with the first of their five babies (Bonnie, Bobby, Betty, Buddy, and Billy) before Billie settled down to homemaking. (She was replaced by Tedd Smith, a gifted alumnus of the Royal Conservatory in Toronto, who has been the Team pianist ever since.)

The Barrows home in Greenville, S.C., called Melody Lane, is Cliff's base for a multitude of activities on Billy Graham's behalf. He is music director for the Billy Graham Evangelistic Association (BGEA). "What Ira D. Sankey was to Dwight Moody and what Homer Rodeheaver was to Billy Sunday," writes one religious journalist, "Cliff Barrows is to Billy Graham and much, much more." He is program director for the "Hour of Decision" and Melody Lane is equipped with a huge tape library and recording studio where choir selections can be spliced into broadcasts. He is in charge of the semi-annual television programs. He is president of BGEA's film studio, World Wide Pictures of Burbank, California—the world's largest maker of religious films, with headquarters a block away from Walt Disney. And, on the Crusade platform, he trains and leads every choir, MC's every service, and is responsible for every event preceding Billy Graham's message.

"We try to present a type of music that has the broadest appeal to the widest segment of the middle-ground audience," Cliff Barrows told me. "It has to be consistent with the theology Mr. Graham preaches and the good taste we feel in music. We don't lean toward the rock-&-roll that a lot of church groups are going to nowadays, but we do try to be as informal, as reverent, and as cheerful as we can.

"You can find a hymn to say anything you're going to say, so long as it's theologically correct, but you can easily pick the wrong hymn for the wrong audience. Tonight, for an evangelistic service geared to the unconverted, I wouldn't pick a staid, sedate hymn like *Holy, Holy, Holy,* which is in our song book. But on Sunday morning, I wouldn't hesitate to use it. Always, we're trying to motivate people to think of Mr. Graham's theme and prepare them for an openness to what Mr. Graham preaches. If I have to cut down on the music or solos or various special introductions, I don't mind in the least. The important thing is the preaching of the word of God and the ministry that God's given Mr. Graham.''

This ruthless self-effacement is why good prayer is the final element of the swiftly-paced 45 minutes that precede Billy Graham. The local clergymen who deliver invocations are carefully scouted and, when necessary, discreetly condensed by Barrows or Walter Smyth, director of Crusade organization and Team activities.

There is also a very discreet ''offering.'' For the first time in evangelistic history, taking up a collection is not one of the feature events. * The most vehement importuning I heard in my nine days of Crusadegoing was a plea by a minister in Ponce for ''a fraction of the daily cost of the war in Vietnam, of what Cassius Clay gets for a minute of fighting Sonny Liston, of the amount that is spent on advertising liquor in Puerto Rico.'' Even then, however, the actual collection was crisp and low-key; it never lasted longer than it took the choir to sing one hymn of redemption.

Underplaying the collection ritual has nothing to do with neglect. It grew out of a crisis that ''came like a kick in the stomach'' to Billy Graham. Prior to 1950, a custom as old as American evangelism itself had been the taking up of a ''love offering'' to pay the preacher. At the end of a six-week Crusade in Atlanta, a local newspaper ran two photos side by side on the front page: one of Billy Graham waving and

---

* In the West End of Louisville less than a decade ago, I witnessed a team of brother evangelists, preaching in a poverty pocket, announcing that they would accept no contributions smaller than $5 bills. ''And just to show that we put our money where our mouth is,'' said the big brother, ''my brother and I are going to start things rolling by putting in $5 apiece of *our own* money.'' They did just that, whereupon little brother took the basket around and brought it back to big brother filled with fivers. The same ritual was then repeated to net hard-earned $1 bills, half-dollars, quarters, and ''petty cash.''

smiling farewell and the other of ushers, grinning from ear to ear and toting four enormous money bags containing the $16,000 "love offering."

"The inference was unmistakable, repeating the old charge that evangelism is a racket," Graham wrote later. "The image of Elmer Gantry was still large in many minds. I remember vowing: This must never happen again . . . However, we faced the question as to how we could finance our work. Our team must have enough to live on and enough for expenses.

"I called Dr. Jesse Bader, Secretary of Evangelism for the National Council of Churches, and asked for his advice. He gave it, and we followed it. He said, 'Incorporate. Have a board of trustees publish the finances, and let the corporation pay all salaries.' For my salary, he named the same sum as . . . the pastor of a large church would receive, $15,000."

Graham heeded Bader and turned the matter over to a Christian businessman named George Wilson, who used to run a religious bookshop in Minneapolis, had organized the first Youth for Christ rally there, and had made the trip to

Taking up an offering is handled unobtrusively.

George M. Wilson (center) publicly deposits a 37-pound black-walnut donation shaped like a map of Tennessee.

England with Graham and the Barrowses. Soon after their return, Graham had joined Wilson at Northwestern Schools, a fundamentalist Bible college in Minneapolis—where Wilson was business manager and Graham became president at the age of 29! (Two years earlier, Graham's predecessor, then 84, had heard him speak at Youth for Christ, pronounced him a "comer," and designated him as his successor.) Graham conducted his new office dynamically, but rather unwillingly and remotely, from 1947 to 1951—largely via long-distance telephone from wherever he was Crusading and via lengthy memos to his faculty. One of these began with the salutation: "Dear Gang: . . ."

George Wilson makes it his business to anticipate crises and so he already had the incorporation papers drawn up when Graham reacted to the Atlanta "love offering" crisis of 1950. Wilson had been unable to interest Graham in incorporating sooner, because the evangelist dreaded becoming a business. But after Atlanta he agreed to the creation of the far-flung Billy Graham Evangelistic Association, which is now a $10-million-a-year organization with headquarters in Minneapolis and offices in London, Paris, Frankfurt, Sydney, Mexico City, Buenos Aires, Winnipeg (on Graham Road), Atlanta, Burbank (World Wide Pictures), Montreat (at the foot of Piney Ridge; staffed by associate evangelist T. W. Wilson and a secretary named Martha Warkentin), Black Mountain, N.C. (where the Association operates radio station WFGW—the first three call letters stand for William Franklin Graham—and WMIT-FM), and Honolulu (radio station KAIM, AM & FM).

In the 19 years since he went on salary, Graham has received just one raise: to $19,500 in 1963: "In addition, I have some small income from my father's estate. He was a poor farmer, but the city moved out on his farm, and he had enough sense to lease some of the land rather than selling all of it. I do not take any income from royalties. * They are put into a trust fund and, should I die, the trustees will decide if my wife needs any funds. If not, the money will go to church work. I also receive a small amount of money for my newspaper column. These are my only sources of income."

---

* Graham's four hard-cover books are *Peace With God* (1953), which has sold 185,936 copies plus another 1,333,000 in paperback as of May 1, 1967; *The Secret of Happiness* (1955) and *My Answer* (1960), both of which had thinner but highly respectable sales; and *World Aflame* (1965) which has sold 271,933 in hard-cover plus 475,000 in a paperback that was published in early 1967. Even though some of these are bought as premiums and given away by the Graham organization, his royalties nonetheless must amount to at least $500,000. While a Billy Graham book often outsells the Number 1 Best Seller of its year, Graham's work seldom spends much time or climbs very high on the best-seller charts, which are confined to bookstore sales *only*. *World Aflame* has been published in Norwegian, Chinese, German, Portuguese, Finnish, Swedish, African, Spanish, Dutch, Japanese, Arabic, and Italian. *Peace With God* has been translated into all of these plus Bahassar Indonesian, Bengali, Danish, Farsi, French, Gujarti, Hindi, Hebrew, Kamarese, Korean, Malayalam, Marathi, Papiamento, Polish, Russian, Serbo-Croat, Tagalog, Telegu, Thai and Ukrainian.

Walter Smyth co-ordinates Crusades from Atlanta base.

(Approximately half of the Billy Graham Evangelistic Association's annual budget is raised from contributions discreetly solicited at the end of the "Hour of Decision" when Cliff Barrows or an announcer purrs: "You are invited to send your free-will gifts and offerings for the support of this program to Billy Graham, Minneapolis, Minnesota. That's all the address you need, just Billy Graham, Minneapolis, Minnesota." Foreigners are particularly perplexed by these phonetics, but letters addressed to "Many Hopeless, Many Soldier" and "Minny Atmos, Minny Soda" have reached—as has mail with no other address but a crude drawing of Billy Graham.)

The Minneapolis *Tribune* has said that "BGEA's appeal rests with the common folk of the world—the children who save a penny each meal for Billy Graham, the shut-in grandmothers who scrape a little from their Social Security checks, the small-town Sunday school teachers. For that reason, the average gift amounts to little more than six dollars."

To which George Wilson, now executive vice-president and treasurer of BGEA, adds: "A $50 contribution is a big one for us."

And a man who was one of the ten to put up $300 apiece to finance that 1949 Los Angeles Crusade in a "Canvas Cathedral" said in 1962: "If I had put the $300 into stock in Litton Industries, it would be worth $75,000 today. But, if I had the same choice to make again and I knew what the financial return would be, I'd do the very same thing all over again."

Long before a Crusade begins, advance men from BGEA help the local sponsors estimate costs. "It's not just one week of a Crusade," Walter Smyth, BGEA's Director of Crusades tells them, "it's at least a year. Your budget begins when you open an office." He will suggest that 50 per cent of the budget be raised in advance from individuals and organizations sympathetic to the cause; the offerings at the meetings tend to match that amount. BGEA stipulates that, at the end of the Crusade, a certified public accountant will audit the books. A copy of this audit MUST be sent to every participating minister and local newspaper. *

Dr. Smyth—a ruddy, bouncy missionary sort who spent his boyhood in Belfast and pronounces his name "Smith"— heads a contingent of 12 advance men who work from a huge "Manual of Crusade Office Operating Procedure" with whole chapters devoted to office planning, bulk mailing, and volunteer recruiting.

From the moment a Crusade invitation is accepted by BGEA, the local sponsors are instructed to form committees, which are immediately placed on a month-by-month timetable leading inexorably to the Crusade. These committees include Finance, Arrangements, Field Work, Counseling, Follow-Up, Ushers, Music, Youth, Prayer, and Visitation. During the year preceding the 1965 Crusade, volunteers paid a call—successful or otherwise—on every home in England to tell the inhabitants that Billy Graham was coming. The volunteers were instructed to "do your work at the door. This is a threshold unit. You needn't go in. Visit every dwelling place. Meet coolness with Christianity. Above all, be brief." Another committee runs Operation Andrew, based on the Scriptural reference to "Andrew findeth his own brother Simon . . . and he brought him to Jesus." Walter Smyth takes it from there: "If a church charters a bus to take its people to our meeting, we suggest that they charter two buses. Each bus is booked to half-capacity and each member is asked to invite an unchurched neighbor. He prays for his neighbor and, if the neighbor has been in any way affected by Mr. Graham's sermon, he can help him along on the bus back."

---

* In *Modern Revivalism,* Professor McLoughlin challenges several audits he studied because "the amount of financial juggling that went on between the local committee, outside donors, the 'Hour of Decision,' and the Billy Graham Evangelistic Association, Inc., was only dimly perceivable in these statistics. No dishonesty was involved, but the accounting was so vague as to leave questions as to who had contributed to what and how it was spent." McLoughlin contends that the "people of Richmond, Va., gave $25,000 and the people of Louisville, Ky., gave $22,000 to help the revival campaign in New York City. Part of the money raised in New York, however, was given to support the revival in San Francisco. Money was raised in Nashville and New Orleans for Graham's evangelistic tour of Europe in 1955 and part of the collections taken at his London crusade in 1954 went to support his crusade in Glasgow a year later."

Several times, while interviewing Walter Smyth, my mind boggled at the pre-planning involved in a Billy Graham Crusade. At one of these moments, Smyth told me: "We believe in organization, but organization must be a means to an end." Then he quoted a Methodist bishop, who once said he "never knew there was anything pious about inefficiency."

All this takes place *after* an invitation is accepted. "We can only accept about one out of a hundred invitations that we receive," Smyth told me. "It takes about five years from an initial invitation until the opening of a Crusade. If the sponsors aren't serious or want us in town for some ulterior motive like a factional or political struggle, their interest will dissipate in that time." Even if interest remains strong, BGEA will investigate the local situation carefully; Smyth paid four preliminary visits to San Juan before accepting the invitation.

Because of the time lag involved, Smyth was able to sketch some fairly definite highlights from Billy Graham's itinerary for the next two years: In 1969 crusades in Auckland, New Zealand, Melbourne and Victoria, Australia. In June of 1969, "barring unforeseen circumstances", he will conduct a month-long New York Crusade in the new Madison Square Garden to be followed by one in California next fall.

Once a local Crusade has opened, BGEA cannot afford to let down its organizational and financial vigilance. At Bithorn Stadium in San Juan one night, nine saintly-looking missionaries, in white gowns and with flowing hair, waited for Billy Graham to come down from his platform. They were the Herbert Dockter Missionary Family (husband, wife, six children ages 3 to 15 *, and one sister) who said they preach a gospel "essentially the same as Mr. Graham's" around the island. They had raised $50 to present to him personally. Before the Dockters could introduce themselves to him, however, Billy Graham swerved and gave them a wide berth. Stan Mooneyham, who works out of Smyth's

---

* When I asked the oldest Dockter girl her age, she replied: "Eternal."

31

Stan Mooneyham: "Mr. Graham can't take money personally."

office in Atlanta, came over to Mrs. Dockter and said softly: "Of course you understand that he cannot accept money personally."

Once the collections and invocations and choral singing are past, the preliminaries have virtually ended. George Beverly Shea sings one last solo—one of 15 solemn hymns about the *person* of Christ (e.g., *I'd Rather Have Jesus*). "Billy," says Shea, "looks forward to the solo before the message as a time for people to quiet down and for him to gather strength."

When Shea sits down, Billy Graham rises and walks to the podium. He wears a white shirt and one of several well-kept brown suits that have earned him the label of "Gabriel in Gabardine." There is no introduction. No introduction is necessary.

Billy Graham begins briskly, like a chairman rushing through committee reports and old business in a headlong rush to confront the issue at hand:

"Yesterday I made a mistake. I said our starting times at night would be 7:30. I should have said every night at 8—every night through Saturday. On Sunday, we will have an Easter Sunrise service at 6 A.M.—six o'clock in the morning on Easter Sunday. Keep this especially in mind. I hope you will bring your friends and let's fill this stadium to overflowing. Now tomorrow night my subject will be 'What's Wrong With the World?' On Wednesday night 'The Problems of Young People.' I want you to get every young person you know to come with you. On Thursday night, I will have another night for young people and I will bring up another kind of problem: 'What Kind of Person Should You Marry?' On Friday night, Good Friday: 'The Scandal of Christianity.' On Saturday, 'How to Have a Happy Home.' I have a happy home. The other day I said I'd been married almost 25 years and now it's like a honeymoon—and a reporter asked me: 'But isn't that abnormal?' And I replied: 'A society must be abnormal that thinks such a condition abnormal.' And it is. In the United States, one marriage in four breaks up. In Los Angeles County, one in two. But, in homes that have Bible-reading, one in 500!"

Doña Felisa, Lady Mayor, opens the San Juan Crusade.

In the fall of 1940, Billy Graham wrote home that he had just met a wonderful girl named Ruth Bell who looked and even sounded like his own mother. This, he said, was the girl he was going to marry.

Graham, then 21, was a newly-enrolled first-year student at Wheaton College in Illinois, a "Bible-centered" institution where he majored in anthropology (and was fed, according to his biographer Professor McLoughlin, the standard Bible Belt teachings—including the staple that the theory of evolution was false). Ruth McCue Bell—a Virginia belle born in North China to missionary parents—was a second-year student. One day, she was passing through Williston Hall when "all of a sudden I heard a voice praying from the next room. I had never heard anyone pray like that before. I knew that someone was talking to God. I sensed that here was a man that knew God in a very special way."

She got to know this man better a few minutes later when a friend introduced them in the lobby. Ruth, who had gone to high school in Korea, was studying to become a missionary to Tibet. Even after accepting Billy's proposal of marriage the following summer, she feared that she might be betraying her missionary calling by becoming a housewife.

"Well, do you think God brought us together?" her fiancé asked.

Ruth Bell had to admit that she felt He had.

Billy then pointed out that the Bible teaches that the husband is the head of the family: "Ruth, the Lord leads me and you follow."

And how could Ruth Bell, of all people, harden her heart to Billy Graham's pleas?

They were married on Friday the 13th of August, 1943, at Montreat—then, as now, a Presbyterian conference center at the foot of Piney Ridge—and honeymooned in a $2-a-day cottage at Blowing Rock in the Blue Ridge Mountains. They had three daughters: Virginia Leftwich, alias "Gigi", now 23 and married; Anne Morrow, now 20 and married; and Ruth Bell, alias "Bunny", now 18 and at school in Long Island. Then they had two sons: Franklin, now 16 and also at school in Long Island, and Nelson Edman "call me Ned, *please,*" 10. Now there are two grandchildren by Gigi's marriage to Stephan Tchividjian, son of a Swiss-Armenian financier. Yes, Billy Graham *is* a grandfather!

His grandchildren are a source of wonderment to him, too. "I hope you have children," he told the Saturday-night throng in San Juan. "I have two grandchildren. They speak French. When they came to visit me, I couldn't understand a word they said. I said to myself, 'Are these my grandchildren?' And yet I loved them. My blood coursed through their veins.''

His first two daughters married young. Gigi was 17. Anne was 18 when she wed Daniel Lotz, a onetime University of North Carolina basketball star. These early marriages did not alarm the Grahams. "It's the *average* age of a couple that's important," Ruth Graham assured me. "Danny was 29 when he married Anne and Stephan was 24 when he married Gigi.''

Ruth Bell Graham is a spunky, determined pioneer-type woman who is as homespun as the rustic mountain retreat she has hewn for her husband. Billy Graham talks of it as "the house that Ruth built" because, while she didn't erect it single-handedly, she conceived and masterminded it while he was in Europe in 1954. Every log in the two-story house is at least 100 years old. For a year, Ruth Graham bought up abandoned log cabins (one of them, she discovered, was still being used by a bootlegger) and left word in filling stations that she was in the market for logs.

Several of the workmen that she hired caused more trouble than they were worth. "All their training," Ruth explained to me, "had taught them that old logs go out of sight. One of them said: 'I can't take no pride in this kind of work.' He quit on us when I gave him some closet doors to hang that he said he wouldn't hang on his chicken coop. The other workmen felt the same way, I think, though they wouldn't say so. But when I began to bring in the old furniture I'd very carefully picked out, you should have seen their faces light up. One of them said, 'It sort of creeps up on you.' ''

The house that Ruth built is U-shaped, with a spinning wheel, geraniums, petunias, and marigolds out front, and a swimming pool down the road. When I asked how many rooms there were, Ruth Graham honestly didn't know: "When all the children are here, there are too few and when they aren't, there are too many rooms." Later, when she showed me around, I counted 11 rooms plus four bathrooms and a couple of attics.

There was a fireplace in almost every room. When I was

there in May, there was always a fire going whenever we sat in the living room and we were never unduly warm. Over the living-room fireplace was a knight's helmet with philodendron growing out of it. It rested on a mantelpiece made from the old diving board down in Montreat. Carved on the mantel in German was ''A Mighty Fortress Is Our God.''

There was a broad-ax over the fireplace of the guest room in which I slept. My bed was a copy of a press bed with a trundle bed underneath—''where our cat had kittens,'' Ruth told me. To get to bed, I had to climb up three steps which, I learned from Ruth the next day, ''used to belong to a casket-maker in Asheville.'' People used to mount the little staircase to view the remains.

The Grahams share a bedroom with doors opening onto a separate study for each. Ruth's study also connects to another bedroom, which is nearer to the base of the house's U-shape. Here she sleeps when she wants to keep an ear out for Ned (and the other children when they're at home) or when her husband is away. In Ruth's study is a whole shelf of C. S. Lewis, ''who stretches my mind,'' and another shelf of Amy Carmichael, an inspirational writer ''who stretches my heart.''

Billy Graham's study, designed by a friend in Greensboro, is at the most distant tip of the U and spills over into the master bedroom. Above the double bed are separate shelves labeled ''OLD TESTAMENT'' and ''NEW TESTAMENT.'' But I gathered that Billy Graham likes to read in bed when I noticed *The Professional,* William S. White's biography of Lyndon Johnson, filed under ''OLD TESTAMENT.''

Billy Graham's generosity is such that, after asking questions about a couple of books and being given his copy of each, I stopped asking. A man who once admired Graham's cufflinks at a social function was handed them on the spot and Graham walked around for the rest of the evening with his sleeves flapping. Early in his career, Graham was addicted to hand-painted ties and, when someone in a British dinner audience remarked upon this, Graham responded, ''You like it? Then it's yours!'' and took it off.

Frank, Anne, Bunny, Ruth, Billy, and Ned Graham.

"She's been with the Queen . . . but she's still Ruth."

The men in the family meet: Ned, Billy, and Frank.

As I toured the house, I perceived hardly any of the ticky-tacky motel plastic that one might expect of a jet-age superevangelist—unless you count the Courtesy Coffee machine I found in my bathroom. The remote-control switch under my pillow for operating lights and TV was a virtual necessity considering the huge room's elevated bed.

Mostly, what I found atop Piney Ridge was unpretentious sophistication and human warmth amidst rough-hewn grandeur. Ruth Graham has made her man a nest where he can relax, study and recharge his batteries with a minimum of high-tension jolts from visiting Messiahs and determined curiosity-seekers. If ever there was a secret of Billy Graham's success—and particularly his durability on the world scene—it is Ruth Graham. One of her Buncombe County neighbors has remarked: "She's been with the Queen, she's been with the President, but Ruth is just Ruth." She has fought quietly but fiercely to keep her husband and her family and her home *simple,* in the best sense of the word.

When I said so a few hours after I'd unpacked my bags, neither of the Grahams demurred, but Ruth simply added: "The pets help, too. Bill's always liked animals. They don't ask anything of him. They just enjoy him and love him and let him love them back. Everyone else—even the children—asks something of him."

At present, two dogs—a St. Bernard and an Alsatian—a cat, and a silent canary (that "got an inferiority complex when Bill said 'hush'," according to Ruth) make the Graham home a Noah's ark of happy confusion. Once upon a time, there were also three Hampshire sheep. I was shown the steep, rocky hillside down which the ram once butted Billy Graham, fracturing his leg.

I had arrived on Friday afternoon, just in time for "Chinese Food Night" at the Billy Grahams'. Friday's Oriental meal and Christmas breakfast's oyster stew are the tangible vestiges of Ruth Graham's mission past. We ate in the "keeping room"—a combined kitchen and living room where, said Ruth, "we do most of our living." The meal was served on a round table with a lazy-Susan center from which you helped yourself to Ruth's sesame beef, Chinese cabbage, egg roll, soy and sweet-and-sour sauces, and rice.

When you were ready for seconds, and in my case, thirds, you simply gave the lazy-Susan a spin.

For the rest of my stay, we ate breakfasts—bacon and eggs and all the trimmings, but no coffee for Billy Graham because of his blood pressure—in the keeping room and lunch in the formal dining room. Saturday lunch was a TV Dinner—"Billy *likes* them," Ruth apologized—preceded by a curried soup and a homemade dessert. Billy Graham considers a meal "something to get through, not something to linger over."

During the Chinese dinner, which Ruth cooked herself (I saw only one servant all weekend, but was told there were two), she told a couple of hilariously grisly stories.

One was from her own girlhood. At the missionary hospital in China, Ruth's father, Dr. L. Nelson Bell, who lives down in Montreat now, needed cadavers for research. He requested several from a Chinese warlord who was conducting wholesale executions some distance away. When the first shipment arrived, the bodies had been so badly tortured and mutilated before execution that they were worse than useless. Dr. Bell fired off an angry complaint. The warlord's reply was to this effect: "O.K. Next time we'll send them alive and *you* execute them."

The other tale was about her older son Franklin's boyhood. More than a dozen years ago, when he was 3 and his father was away, Franklin found a cigarette. "He insisted he wanted to smoke it," said Ruth, "and I started to take it away from him. But then I remembered that this was one sure way to make smoking look appealing. So I said, 'All right, Franklin. You can smoke it, but only if you smoke it to the very end.' Well, that's exactly what Franklin did and then he asked for another. After the second cigarette, I called over one of the workmen and asked for his advice. He had Franklin smoke another and said that Franklin wasn't inhaling; I should make him inhale. I told Franklin he'd have to inhale and he did. Then he finished that one and asked for another. From there, he ran into the bathroom and threw up. Then he came back, smoked some more, and threw up some more.

"This continued into the evening and the workman came

back after dinner to see how we were doing. The kitchen looked like an opium den with the three of us sitting around the table and Franklin smoking and excusing himself and then coming back.

"I don't know how many cigarettes he smoked. But finally, when he could hardly keep his eyes open, he looked at me and said: " 'Aw Mom, y'know I'm not gonna smoke when I grow up.' "

". . . And on Sunday morning, our last service. Let's make it the greatest Easter sunrise service ever. Now I'm going to ask tonight that everyone be quiet, everyone be reverent. My message will be brief, so you listen. It will change many destinies in here tonight. Now the Bible says you have two sets of ears. You have physical ears that you hear with. But you also have a soul and your soul has ears. While I'm speaking to you, God will be speaking to your soul. So let us have no walking around, no talking, no whispering. One person moving can disturb everyone around him. Now tonight I know it's drizzling. I am not a prophet of rain, but I don't think it will last very long. If it rains harder, some of you will have to put up your umbrellas. But be as quiet as you can. If He could hang on the Cross for us, certainly we can stand a few drops of rain for Him. Once in a while during my message, we may have a jet plane come over. When the plane comes over, I'll stop for a minute—so you don't miss anything. Because I want you to listen like you've never listened to anything before in your life. What you hear tonight in the rain may change your life. It may well determine where you'll be a hundred years from now."

He commands and we obey—not only because the same admonitions hush us night after night, but also because he is Billy Graham who commands, in varying degrees, our interest, our respect, our reverence. He has ranked high on the Gallup Poll's list of the Ten Most Admired Men in the World every year from 1951 onward. He has been officially honored, on numerous occasions, as Clergyman of the Year, Salesman of the Year, Speaker of the Year, Big Brother of the Year, and *Time's* Man of the Year. According to his press clipping service he makes more news items than any other person living in the world today except That Man in the White House. Last year, he dictated or wrote replies to 11,000 letters—a tiny fraction of the mail that is addressed to him. Three thousand of these answers were to speaking invitations deemed urgent enough to be forwarded to him by his various offices. Almost all were declined. (When he does speak, he donates his customary $5,000 fee to the Easter Seal Fund or some other philanthropy.)

Billy Graham has preached to more people in more parts of the world than any man dead or alive. Statistics and headlines tell some of the story: 122,000 FILL WEMBLEY IN THE RAIN; 134,254 IN LOS ANGELES COLISEUM WITH 20,000 OVERFLOW OUTSIDE; 116,000 PACK SOLDIER FIELD IN 100-DEGREE CHICAGO HEAT; 75,000 IN COTTON BOWL TO HEAR GRAHAM; 143,750 AT MELBOURNE CRICKET GROUND. He outdrew Pope Paul at Yankee Stadium and bloodless bullfights in the Astrodome. Total attendance at his Crusades is more than 35 million and in 1966 the ranks of converts swelled past the 1-million mark. He has preached in person to naked African tribesmen and British royalty (whose elegant footman, reaching for Graham's hat, received a hearty handshake instead). He has delivered his message at the Brandenburg Gate, accompanied by a choir recruited from West and East Berlin. Every Sunday, some 25-million people around the world hear him on the "Hour of Decision." Every day, at least 200 people come forward to stand before movie screens and make "decisions for Christ" after watching one or another of the 84 World Wide Pictures, most of which feature a "Special Appearance" by Billy Graham. In the jungles of Fiji and New Guinea, natives crouch in village compounds to hear tapes of Billy Graham with live missionaries translating him into pidgin. But, when the British Broadcasting Corporation asked Graham, "What is your total worldwide following?", his answer was: "*My* total following? I hope none. I work for Christ."

Skeptics have scoffed at "The Pied Piper of the Pulpit"

and called him "a strange new junction of Madison Avenue and the Bible Belt." To this Graham replies: "I'm selling the greatest product in the world. Why shouldn't it be promoted as well as soap?"

He is, at the very least, an item of Americana—as witness his frequent appearances in the pages of *Reader's Digest.* Governor John Connally of Texas, speaking just three weeks before his ride through Dallas with President Kennedy, said that "Billy Graham is more than a preacher, more than an evangelist, more than a Christian leader. In a greater sense, he has become our conscience."

In recent years, Graham has endured and enjoyed the epithet of "White House Chaplain"—swimming partner of LBJ, golf partner of JFK, and unofficial spiritual guide to Ike. Once, he was summoned from a shower at Burning Tree Country Club to chat with President Eisenhower and Vice-President Nixon in the dressing room. Nixon remarked that Graham was "probably the only preacher in history to talk to the President and Vice-President at the same time, dressed only in a towel."

"The Eisenhower era was a time of spiritual awakening in America," said Billy Graham in 1964 ."The example he gave contributed much to this revival. He was always faithful in church attendance, come rain or shine. Under him, I believe Americans felt a degree of security unknown under other Presidents." As a close friend of Dick Nixon, Graham felt in the 1960 campaign that Nixon would make a better President than Jack Kennedy. But Nixon urged him not to come out for him publicly "because your ministry is more important than my getting elected President." In 1968, however, Graham was highly visible as a member of Nixon's brain trust.

The religious statesman of today has come a long way from the unpolished Boy Evangelist in loud tie and white buckskin shoes who once outraged Harry Truman by kneeling on the White House lawn to show the press photographers how he had just prayed with the President . . . who told the Queen of England that "it looks like your parks have been turned into bedrooms" . . . and who suggested that if the United States gave Prime Minister Nehru a streamlined train or a pure white Cadillac, it "would do more to demonstrate the friendliness of the Americans than all the millions of dollars given in economic aid" to India.

In public, in private, and in print, many who came to scoff have remained to pray, including the proverbial "people in high places." Although the identities of Graham's converts are seldom divulged, they do "come forward" in public and so the big names rarely remain secret. On opening day in San Juan, the lady Mayor, Doña Felisa Rincón de Gautier left the platform in tears to join the stream of inquirers coming forward. In 1966, when Hayley Mills' parents brought her to hear Billy Graham, their gifted but troubled daughter surprised everybody by coming forward. Later, her parents took her to a private meeting with Billy Graham.

"She flew right into my arms and kissed me," Graham reported. "And her parents thanked me."

"Making the decision for God was like opening the front door and filling my lungs with fresh, clean air," Hayley confided to *Motion Picture* Magazine, which cover-lined the interview as "HOW BILLY GRAHAM LED HAYLEY MILLS BACK TO GOD."

Partly because backsliding converts can give an evangelist a bad name and largely because there are elements of sanctity and privacy even in public conversion, BGEA will not give out names for publications. But that first 1949 Los Angeles Crusade's converts included Lou Zamperini, the Olympic track star and war hero who now runs a Christian boys' camp for juvenile delinquents; Jim Vaus, who used to be gangster Mickey Cohen's chief wiretapper and is now Executive Director of Youth Development, Inc., in New York City; and Stuart Hamblen, a cowboy actor who later wrote the song *It Is No Secret What God Can Do.* And it is no secret that subsequent West Coast Crusades have brought forward Roy Rogers, Dale Evans, and Dick Van Dyke as upturned faces in the crowd. Some big names, in fact, became so identified with Graham's cause that Dick Van Dyke later felt impelled to caution an interviewer: "Don't run off with the idea I'm a kind of Hollywood version of Billy Graham. I'm not. In fact, I'm utterly opposed to a lot of his teaching."

45

In a television interview just before the 1957 New York Crusade opened, Ethel Waters was asked: "Don't you think Graham is over-reaching himself trying to fill Madison Square Garden?" The actress shook her head and said: "God don't sponsor no flops."

On opening night, she made an even deeper commitment when she came forward to rededicate her life to Christ: "I felt that my Lord was calling me back home." Today, nearing 70, Ethel Waters lends her voice (*His Eye Is on the Sparrow*) to as many Billy Graham Crusades as she can get to.

Jimmy Karam, a football coach and reported segregationist, was charged by the Mayor of Little Rock in the New York *Times* with having instigated the Arkansas capital's 1957 race riots.* He later turned up as a Crusade helper when Billy Graham visited Arkansas and now, having broken with his segregationist cronies, preaches the gospel. In his death cell, Carl Hall, the St. Louis police lieutenant who kidnapped and killed Bobby Greenlease, was converted by reading *Peace With God*.

"In 1961 in England," Billy Graham told me, "the Crown Prince of another country came forward and accepted Christ. Later, he became the king.† In another country the ruler's grandchildren were among the inquirers. Still another who came forward is now Head of State of an African nation. . . . And in Great Britain, many who were saved in our 1954 Crusade are now clergymen there."

Perhaps the ultimate symbol of Billy Graham's rise in universal esteem was the stiletto pen of the London *Daily Mirror's* fearsome "Cassandra," alias Sir William Connor. In 1954, Cassandra had warned this "hot gospeller" to stay away from England's shores. But Graham came and conquered and even met "Cassandra" in a public house called The Baptist's Head. "Cassandra" found him "a teetotaler and abstainer able to make himself completely at his ease in the spit and sawdust department; which is, in my view, a difficult thing to do."

The two men became firm friends and pen pals until Connor's recent death. "I never thought that friendliness

---

*Karam denied this charge. †Still later, he was deposed.

had such a sharp cutting edge," Connor wrote. "I never thought that simplicity could cudgel us sinners so damned hard." In 1966, "Cassandra" welcomed Graham back to Britain under the banner headline of "WE KNOW AND LOVE YOU, BILLY." And he was not alone. The *Daily Mail* proclaimed: "WE'VE GROWN ACCUSTOMED TO HIS FAITH."

"Now I want you all to bow your heads. My associate evangelist, Dr. Vangioni, will lead us in prayer and then I will speak on 'The Wickedest Man Who Ever Lived.'"

A dapper Argentinian with thinning silver hair and an arthritic limp hobbles to the pulpit. As co-ordinator of Billy Graham Crusades in Latin America, Fernando Vangioni has spearheaded the advance thrust through all of Puerto Rico plus the Virgin Islands and Aruba. The nightly crowds in San Juan, ranging from 8,000 to 17,500, were a tribute to his groundwork. For weeks and months, a web of pre-Crusades had criss-crossed the islands—paving the way for Billy Graham, organizing airport welcomes in Ponce and San Juan, and chartering buses and planes for expeditions to the San Juan Crusade. The Rev. Pablo Finkenbinder had preached in Cayey, Aguadilla, and Ponce; the Rev. José D. Camacho in Fajardo, Humacao, and Guayama. And Fernando Vangioni had addressed crowds in the outlying islands, at schools and universities, and in the cities of Arecibo, Mayaguez, and Bayamon, as well as for two weeks in Ponce. Vangioni, considered the world's greatest Spanish-speaking evangelist, was a fiery prelude to Billy Graham's one night visit to Ponce.

The results had been highly impressive for Protestants in predominantly Catholic territory. Couples who had been living out of wedlock for years—parents and grandparents —had come forward to make "decisions for Christ" and followed through by appearing in church on Sunday to ask to be married. At the Inter-American University branch in Ponce, 150 students had come to hear Vangioni preach on campus—and 100 of them, plus two professors, had stood up to make commitments to Christ. In Arecibo, ten men listening to Vangioni on a transistor radio had been converted on the spot; they knelt and prayed and then climbed into one car and sought out a pastor. In Bayamon, a convert who came forward had handed to his counsellor a loaded pistol that he would no longer need; he had planned to kill himself. Drunkards had reformed; dope addicts had sought help; and the resulting headlines and gossip were the talk of all Puerto Rico.

The only misfire in generating this climate of excitement had been an airdrop of 25,000 leaflets over Ponce. Treacherous currents had borne all but a handful of paper upward into the surrounding mountains—prompting one local skeptic to rejoice in scientific proof that "hot air rises!"

I had arrived in Ponce in time for the last three nights of Vangioni's pre-Crusade and had, in fact, breakfasted with him on my hotel balcony. He had told me of his initial contact with Billy Graham as his translator in Buenos Aires, where Dr. and Mrs. Vangioni had a television program called "A Moment of Meditation." Later, Vangioni had been flown up to the States to sit in on a Team meeting, at which he was invited to join.* "I remember," Vangioni told me, "that before we knelt, Billy Graham said to us: 'Pray for me that I shall not be considered even a great preacher or a great evangelist, but pray for me that I will always be a man of God.' And that impressed me much."

Vangioni's sermons, too, had impressed me much. He laced them with sordid references to Sodom, Gomorrah, Babylon, and Los Angeles. He ticked off sins, scandals, and disasters like tabloid headlines. At one point, he cried out: "What do we call Christianity today? People who dare to call themselves Christians are also robbers! *Adulterers!* FORNICATORS! Liars! They have children without names. They violate all Ten Commandments. Is this Christianity? NO!" The parables he related were equally sensational. He told of the master who stamped his servant to death and atoned by rearing his orphaned son as his own and educating him as an artist—only to have him paint the

---

* The Team, at last count, numbered 46 of the key executives, aides and associate evangelists of BGEA.

scene of his father's murder. He claimed that Ponce de Leon himself (after whom the city of Ponce is named) spent his life searching for the Fountain of Youth only to find that the wellspring was in the New Testament itself. He mentioned the rich man whose wealth cannot buy him one extra minute of life and listed a cavalcade of villains who entered scoffing and exited praying. Every tale was dished out like a jeweled icicle of blood seasoned with a torrid Spanish Gothic relish.

I had only one reservation about Vangioni's performance —and it was that each message had a tricky ending. At the end, he asked us to bow our heads. Then he asked all who prayed with him and believed with him to raise their hands.

Evangelists Vangioni & Graham wait side-by-side to pray.

Most of the crowd responded. Then he asked those with their hands in the air to stand at their seats. Most did. Then he asked all those who were standing to come forward. At this point, a number of people sat down hard. Others remained standing. Of the impressive number that actually moved forward, one could suspect that not all of them realized they were about to be converted, interviewed, and enrolled in a follow-up correspondence course in Bible study.

Therefore, I was greatly relieved when Billy Graham came to Ponce and gave an absolutely straightforward invitation (as he did every night in San Juan, too):

"I'm going to ask you to get up out of your seat right now and come and stand in front of this platform and say by coming, 'I receive Christ. . .' And after you come we're going to give you some Scripture, some literature, have a moment of prayer, and you can go back and join your friends. If you're with a friend, bring your friend with you. But I'm going to ask you to come quickly. Hundreds of you. Men. Women. Young people. You come. Just get out of your seat and come and stand here quietly. . ."

Seeing Graham after Vangioni reminded me of the old Brooklyn Dodgers when big Don Newcombe and crafty Preacher Roe were their pitching aces. After eight brilliant innings, one would seem to need a spitball to survive the ninth. It was a joy the next night to watch the other blaze through nine innings with the greatest of ease.

Speaking of the response Graham evokes, Walter Smyth of his Team once said: "The one great gift that God has given to Billy Graham is the gift of the invitation. There is no *earthly* reason for those people to come forward, but they do."

A religious writer, who has seen virtually the entire Team in action at one place or another, said: "Graham's brother-in-law, Leighton Ford, gives a better-structured sermon, but the people come forward for Billy Graham. All the others have to coax."

Billy Graham told me: "I've always felt that what little sovereign gift I have is at that moment."

> *"I want you to turn with me, if you will, to the 21st Chapter of Second Kings. Now if you have any difficulty finding Second Kings, it comes right after First Kings [the audience titters] and right before First Chronicles.*
>
> *" 'Manasseh was 12 years old when he began to reign and he reigned fifty-and-five years in Jerusalem.' Then is given an account of one of the most vicious, the most vile, and the most evil of all men. I doubt if there has been a man who has been more wicked in the history of the world than was the King of Judah by the name of Manasseh. Everything evil you can think of—murder,*

50

adultery, torture—he was guilty of it. The Bible says he
would sit down and try to think of new ways to do evil.
"His father was Hezekiah, one of the great and good
kings of Judah. . . . Now comes his son, and his son
undid all that his father had tried to accomplish. That is
true many times in history. Sometimes parents leave a
great spiritual heritage and their children wander away
from it. Perhaps YOUR mother and father were Chris-
tians. They followed Christ, they were faithful in the
church, they were loyal to the precepts of the teachings
of Christ in their daily living, but YOU have neglected
God! You have neglected Christ! You are living only for
yourself!"

Billy Graham's father, William Franklin Graham, Sr.,
was a devout Presbyterian who had longed in his youth for
the Lord to "call" him into the ministry. The call never
came and the elder Graham settled instead for a 200-acre
dairy farm in Sharon Township on the outskirts of Charlotte, N. C. His wife, Morrow, prayed that this call would be
granted to their firstborn son, whom everybody knew as
"Billy Frank."

The Billy Graham we know was born November 7, 1918,
four days before the Armistice that ended World War I.
Young Billy Frank grew up fast; "borrowed" his dad's car
to race it over country roads and even along one city side-
walk; and once termed the religious books his mother read
to her family "all hogwash." But his upbringing was strict:
"If I broke a rule, believe me, Father never hesitated. Off
came his belt. Mother preferred a long hickory switch. But
I always knew they loved me—even while they spanked me.
And that meant more to me than anything else I know."

A veteran of "literally hundreds of whippings," Billy
Graham told an audience in Puerto Rico: "I remember the
first cigarette I ever smoked. Now my father smoked. He
smoked big nickel cigars. But he didn't want his children to
smoke. He fired the man who had given me the cigarette—
one of the workers on the farm. And he spanked me for
twenty minutes. I lost all taste for cigarettes."

When Prohibition was repealed, his father bought a case

of beer and forced him to drink it all until he got sick. He lost all taste for spirits.

Billy Frank was taught that laziness ranked among the worst of evils: "When I was 12 years old, I had to get up at 3 A.M. to milk cows. Every morning before I went to school, I milked twenty cows and every afternoon when I came home from school I had to milk the same twenty cows. I still have a strong grip."

On the Sharon High School baseball team, the rangy youth was a weak-hitting, good-fielding first baseman. He was constantly falling in and out of love. Later, he wrote: "The reasons I didn't commit sexual immorality when the opportunity became so available in my teens is because my parents expected us [there were three younger children] to be clean and never doubted that we would be. They trusted us and made us want to live up to their confidence."

The official Billy Graham attitude toward what his interpreter called "El Sexo" was outlined at his first Youth Night in San Juan:

"Now there's no sin in sex. It was given to you by God. But we've taken something holy and pure and corrupted it. There are four reasons why God discourages immorality. First, to protect your marriage—your *future* marriage. Psychologists tell us that if you are bad boys and bad girls now, it affects your married life later. Second, to protect your body. In spite of all the modern medicines, there are more unwed mothers, more venereal disease, than we've ever had before. Why? Because you sin against the body. Third, to protect you psychologically. And fourth, to protect society. The society that breaks the Commandments destroys itself."

Further elaboration of Graham's views on this subject is found in a World Wide Picture called *The Restless Ones:*

"The Bible takes no hush-hush attitude toward sex. God gave it to us to be used wisely. . . . It's a creative dynamo —the power to create life, *but only within normal bounds.* It's normal to have sex hunger, but man is separated from the animals by his ability to say no . . . [*As for petting*]

You touch the light switch, the lights are going to come on." *

It was, oddly enough, a crisis in sexual immorality that first answered Billy Frank's mother's prayers and brought her son to Christ. In 1934, when Billy Frank was just turning 16, a fire-breathing evangelist named Mordecai Ham came to Charlotte. Ham preached on local issues and scandals— naming names from his pulpit. One night, he shocked his audience by proclaiming that adultery was being committed right *inside* Central High School in Charlotte! The next night, he insisted that it was taking place in the high-school auditorium. And the next night, he produced a teen-age student—one of Ham's recent converts—who repented publicly for having had intercourse behind the assembly platform with several students and one married teacher!

Each night, delegations of irate citizens and mobs of howling teen-agers converged on Ham's raw-pine tabernacle with avowed intentions of beating him up, tarring-and-feathering him, and running him out of town. Each night, confronted by his sincerity and the accuracy of his information, they stayed to pray.

Knowing some of the people involved in the scandal, Billy Frank and two friends—the brothers T. W. and Grady Wilson, no relation to George Wilson—went to find out what Ham was all about.

"I don't recall what Mordecai Ham preached about that night, but I remember that I sat spellbound," Billy Graham wrote later. "The fascination of an old fashioned revival is hard to explain to anybody who never experienced one. The crowd seems to be gripped by a unity of consecration that was much more intense than during regular services. Each listener became deeply involved with the evangelist, who had an almost embarrassing way of describing your sins and shortcomings and demanding, on pain of Divine Judgment, that you mend your ways. As I listened, I began to

---

* For still further details, consult a 60-page paperback called *Billy Graham Talks to Teen-Agers,* by Billy Graham © 1958, Miracles Unlimited, Wheaton, Ill.

have thoughts I had never known before. Something began to speak to my heart.''

He squirmed and twisted and ducked and dodged and resisted, but he kept coming back night after night. For Mordecai Ham, like the best evangelists before and since, seemed to be speaking to *you*. One night, hoping to escape the preacher's piercing eyes and long, accusing finger, Billy Frank sat behind a lady with a high hat. On the night he surrendered to Christ, Billy Frank at first sought sanctuary in the choir: ''I couldn't sing, but at least I'd be safe behind his back.'' But Ham preached: ''He that being often reproved and hardeneth his neck shall suddenly be cut off . . . without remedy'' and the choir began to sing *Just As I Am Without One Plea*. Several hundred worshippers gathered before the pulpit. When the choir switched to *Almost Persuaded, Christ to Believe*, Billy Frank ''could stand it no longer and simply went forward. It was not just the technique . . . It was Christ. I was conscious of Him.''

For most of his life, he has kept his relationship to God and Christ *that* simple.

His friends, Grady and T. W. Wilson, were fellow Fuller Brush Men with Billy Graham in the summer of 1936.* Although it was a Depression year, Billy Graham was netting $50 to $75 a week in commissions—and he was not yet 18!

''Billy was the most dedicated salesman the Fuller Brush Company ever had,'' Grady Wilson assured me. ''That same sincerity has gotten into his Christian work and sells itself around the world.''

Billy Graham says: ''I had become convinced that Fuller brushes were the best in the world and no family should be

---

* Grady Wilson came forward the same night that Graham did; T. W., alias Thomas Walter, didn't convert until a few years later. Both brothers are now Billy Graham's most trusted aides and associate evangelists. T. W., who looks like Bob Hope, handles Graham's appointments and Montreat office and is his traveling companion and frequent chauffeur; he is also president of Graham's Blue Ridge Broadcasting Corp. in North Carolina and chairman of the board of his Christian Broadcasting Corporation of Hawaii. Grady is vice-president of BGEA, substitute speaker when Billy Graham is ill or unavailable, and a recording star in his own right (*Grady Wilson Reads the Bible*).

Boyhood chum Grady Wilson (with envelope) is Graham's greeter.

without them. Selling those brushes became a cause to me
. . . a matter of principle.''

The authorized biography of Billy Graham—by an Angli-
can clergyman named John Pollock—provides two gas-
station glimpses of the teenage salesman in the throes of
first love with the Gospel: In one scene, a garage attendant,
changing a tire, hammered his own thumb by mistake and
swore ''Christ!'' Billy Graham warned him never to do that
again. The garageman had to be restrained from hammer-
ing Graham . . . At another garage, the attendant was filling Graham's jalopy with gas when the young *evangelizer*
leaned over and began: ''Mister, I want to tell you what
happened to me back in Charlotte a couple of years ago . . .''
The response to this aggressive witnessing is not recorded.

As a theology student, however, Billy Graham found the
iron discipline at Bob Jones College, then in Tennessee, too
somber for his taste. He dropped out when he went home for
his first Christmas vacation. Dr. Bob Jones, the Methodist
founder and evangelist, warned him: ''If you're a misfit
here, Billy, you'll be a misfit anywhere.'' (Years later, Bob
Jones, who disapproved of BGEA's lack of affiliation with
any one denomination, was to proclaim that ''Billy Graham
has done more harm to the cause of Christ than any man in

history." His son, Bob Jones, Jr., was also to denounce Graham, but Billy Graham was to turn the other cheek: "I really do love Bob Jones, Senior, and Junior, too."

Early in 1937, Billy Graham entered the Florida Bible Institute, an informal school near Tampa that was affiliated with the World Christian Fundamentals Association. The Institute also doubled as a Bible conference center and resort hotel. A few hours after Billy Graham had checked in, the hotel caterer asked him to take a carload of tourists on a sightseeing tour of Tampa. Graham had never been to Tampa, but "I took them anyway and spent the afternoon explaining the virtues of Tampa, which I didn't know anything about. When I brought them back, they all seemed happy."

He remembers his three-and-a-half years there fondly, even though they involved a roughing-up and a breaking-up. Preaching the gospel in front of a Tampa saloon, he was knocked down by a bartender whose customers then "ground my face in gutter filth." Wooing a girl, he proposed, she said yes and then she changed her mind. Two biographies differ about *why*. One says she "threw him over...because she felt he lacked religious purpose." The other says she fell in love with one of his best friends, whom she *did* marry. In any event, Billy Graham wrote to a classmate that the stars had fallen out of his sky and there was nothing more to live for now that he and she had broken up.

It was not long thereafter at Florida Bible Institute that Billy Graham received the "call" his mother had been praying for. In early 1938, at Swann Lake in northern Florida, he had preached his first church sermon. He had prepared four outlines, chosen one, and then stood up before a congregation of 40 Baptists. It is a matter of interest that Graham was born a Presbyterian and still was one in 1938. A year later, preaching near Palatka, Fla., he was asked before a sermon which Baptist church he belonged to back home. He replied that he was a Presbyterian. The pastor was concerned: "If my deacons find out you're not a Baptist, there may be such an uproar that we'll have to stop these meetings." A few hours later, Graham phoned home and said "I have prayed about this, and I want to become a Baptist." His mother said, "If you feel the Lord is leading you, go ahead." The following Sunday, he was immersed in Silver Lake near Palatka . . . His wife, Ruth, however, is still a staunch Presbyterian. Graham says: "In the early days, we laughed about it, and I would frankly have preferred for her to become a Baptist. If I had asked her, she would have become one; but I didn't. Later, I realized that her conviction was an asset to me . . . As a result of my contact with Presbyterians, people began to see that I wasn't just a narrow be-dipped-or-be-damned Baptist."

Harking back to that very first sermon in Swann Lake, Graham has written: "As I began, my knees shook and my hands and brow became wet. I raced through my first sermon outline, then the second, then the third. At the end of eight minutes, I had gone through all four sermons. I sat down. Nobody ever failed more ignominiously. The experience convinced me that I was not called to preach."

This was the state of mind he was in, one March night, when he went for a walk on the golf course surrounding Florida Bible Institute: "The trees were loaded with Spanish moss and in the moonlight it was like a fairyland. As I stepped onto the fringe of the 18th green, I remember feeling that, despite all arguments to the contrary, God did want me to preach."

Billy Graham says he argued out loud with the Lord: "I can't preach. I couldn't learn to preach. I don't want to preach. No church would have me."

"God," says Graham, "talked right back: 'I can use you. I need you. You make the choice. I will find the place.' "

Toward midnight, Graham recalls, he fell to his knees on the 18th green and said: "All right, Lord, if You want me You've got me."

And so he practiced preaching—at the swampy edge of the Hillsboro River with a cypress stump for a pulpit and alligators for an audience. When visiting preachers came to the school, he re-created and practiced their every mannerism for the uncritical alligators. He borrowed some gestures, discarded others, but mostly he preached like the preacher he knew best—Mordecai Ham.

Later in life, at the end of his own career, Mordecai Ham sent Billy Graham a letter that began (as Graham recollects it):

> I'm an old man. I've made many mistakes in evangelism that I hope you won't make. First, *don't fight the church*. I wish I hadn't been so harsh on the local ministers. I skinned them snout to tail, but this eventually killed my own ministry. Second, *my follow-up of converts was next to nothing*. Third, *hold less meetings and do more studying than I have done*. Fourth, *I used to go into town and deliberately raise an issue and name names to get the attention of the community. That was wrong.* Fifth, *don't put as much emphasis on finances as we did.* We used to have collections that lasted half an hour. And *don't ride hobby horses.* I preached too much on prophecy. Keep to preaching the Gospel, the good news of Christ, and don't get involved in speculating about the future. . . .

Graham, as you have seen or will see, has scrupulously eschewed all these pitfalls. But even as the super-smooth 1969-model Billy Graham purrs along the airways extolling the Greatest Product Ever Sold (one critic has said that Graham's radio message is "Why not try God?") he is not without echoes of Mordecai Ham trudging down the old sawdust trail. On the "Hour of Decision" (which is actually a half-hour broadcast) Billy Graham's sermon on "carnal Christians" began with this Ham-like tidbit: "I even heard about one church where immorality has been taking place during the evening young people's meetings. May God help us!"

> *"Manasseh . . . betrayed everything his father ever left him. He was guilty first of idolatry. Not only was Manasseh guilty of idolatry himself, but he made all other people in the nation worship idols . . .*
>
> *"I tell you today that we in this generation are just as guilty of idolatry as they were in those days. Our gods are no longer made with hands. Idolatry means when we put self over against God. Anything that comes between you and God is YOUR god!*

Graham reads at least 3 hours a day — non-fiction only.

> "The Bible says that covetousness is idolatry. You can
> be covetous. And money becomes your god. Drink be-
> comes your god. Many of us worship social prestige and
> standing. Many of us worship security. We worship ma-
> terial things. Material things are more important to us
> than God! Many of us worship pleasure and entertain-
> ment. We put all those things before God. We spend more
> time watching television than we spend reading the Bible.
> Now there's nothing wrong with watching television. I
> don't say you shouldn't watch it. But when we sit in
> front of the TV set and we get quiet as though we were
> worshipping before it, THEN WE ARE GUILTY OF
> IDOLATRY!"

On a fairly routine Sunday night in New York City
(April 23, 1967), the average radio-and-TV worshipper
might have listened to the omnipresent Billy Graham
throughout the evening.

From 7 to 7:30 P.M., the "Hour of Decision" was on
radio station WOR—and again from 10 to 10:30 P.M. on
WNBC and from 11 to 11:30 P.M. on WABC. All three half-
hours of decision were identical: "Where is the church
when a labor-union leader can defy the law . . . when business tycoons manipulate prices . . . when almost porno-
graphic films are shown on the screen . . . when the Supreme Court, in one decree after another, sweeps the Bible
from our schools?"

To fill in the lull between 10:30 and 11 P.M., the dial-
twirler could have switched on his TV set, found Channel
11, and caught Billy Graham being interviewed about Viet-

nam on "The Bible Study Hour": "I think that today we have a totally different soldier than we had in Korea . . . The men in Vietnam are much more committed. They are better motivated."

A couple of Tuesdays earlier, "CBS Reports" had nationally televised an hour-long BBC documentary on Graham called "I Want You to Get Up Out of Your Seats." On Good Friday in Puerto Rico, anyone not actually attending the Billy Graham Crusade was exposed to three different Billy Graham sermons on the island's otherwise limited TV programming.

Electronic evangelism was first introduced to Billy Graham in 1950 by Walter F. Bennett of Chicago and Fred Dienert of Philadelphia, partners in the Bennett Advertising Agency and specialists in religious accounts ("Light and Life," "The Lutheran Hour," etc.). They button-holed him in Northern Michigan and said they thought he was a natural for a weekly network radio program. Fearing that this could all too easily become a full-time job, Graham brushed them off politely. A few weeks later, they reappeared in Montreat with the news that a peak Sunday hour would soon be available on ABC at a rate of $92,000 for the first 13 weeks. The sum, at the time, impressed Graham as astronomical. He sent them away again.

A little later, preceded by a barrage of telegrams and phone calls, Dienert and Bennett appeared at Graham's Crusade in Portland, Oregon. Breaking down the network cost to $7,000 per program, they explained that he could go on the air for a mere $25,000; after three weeks, they were sure, contributions from listeners would provide enough to sustain the program. Graham again said no and began to shun the two ad men like twin plagues. If he knew they were sitting in ambush in his hotel lobby, he would exit by the rear elevator or fire escape.

When, however, two Texans he knew—a grocery heir named Butt and a bakery owner named Mead—pledged $1,000 apiece to set up a radio fund, Graham summoned Bennett and Dienert to his hotel room. He was wearing, they remember, pajamas and a golf cap—the latter to keep his hair straight. (Graham has also undergone cosmetic dentistry to brighten his smile.) He told them of the pledges and suggested that they might contact other wealthy men. Dienert and Bennett, however, didn't think the money was going to come from a handful of rich men. They suggested that Graham tell the Portland audience about the opportunity.

Billy Graham knelt by his bed and sought God's will by putting out what he called a "Gideon's fleece":

"Lord, You know I'm doing all that I can. You know I don't have any money, but I believe we ought to do this. You know, Lord, I have a mortgage on that little house in Montreat. Lord, I'll put another mortgage on; I'll take the little I have and put another mortgage on. Lord, I don't know where the money is, and if I did know where it is, I'm too busy to go out and get it. I feel the burden for it, but it's up to You, and if You want this, I want You to give me a sign. And I'm going to put out the fleece. And the fleece is for $25,000 by midnight."

That night—after telling his audience that the radio time should be taken for God rather than cigarette advertising— Billy Graham took up a special collection that added an additional $21,500 to his $2,000 radio fund. Over oyster stew at Louie's-on-the-Alley, Graham informed Dienert and Bennett that the fleece had fallen short.

The two partners offered to put up the $1,500 balance, but Graham refused. Morose and silent, they all wandered back to the hotel a few minutes before midnight.

At the front desk were three additional pledges totaling $1,500.

The first "Hour of Decision" went out to 150 stations on Sunday, November 5, 1950. Billy Graham consciously modeled himself after two other Sunday-night radio giants, Walter Winchell and Drew Pearson. His formula involved rapid-fire delivery with frequent examples from current events mixed with Biblical for-instances and quotations: "Fast, hard-hitting . . . straight evangelism calculated to stir the Christian and win the person outside the church to Christ."

His number of outlets has since increased sixfold. The "Hour of Decision" has also served to keep Graham on his toes looking for fresh material. Unlike most peripatetic preachers, he cannot get by with re-using the same sermon in different places every Sunday. His radio half-hour does have a repeated ritual of its own, however. It invariably ends with Graham's bucolic benediction of "God bless you real good" or "May the Lord bless you real good." When I asked Graham about this on the beach in Puerto Rico, he said somewhat apologetically: "I know it's not good grammar, but the one time I stopped using it, people wrote in."

In 1952 and 1953, Billy Graham also had a Sunday half-hour on ABC-TV, but it dwindled to 15 minutes and then disappeared entirely. Overexposure and studio stiffness were blamed, but the actual reason seems to have been network queasiness about what the TV trade calls "commercial religion."

In recent years, Dienert and Bennett have found it most economical and effective to buy TV time from some 300 individual stations across the country rather than from their parent networks. The semi-annual Billy Graham TV effort is concentrated on a late Spring week just before the summer replacements start and a late summer week just after they end. During each of those weeks, local TV may carry three or four or even five nights of Billy Graham meetings videotaped at an actual Crusade. August's was from London; June's was from Winnipeg.

In 1966 in London, the Graham organization experimented with closed-circuit television to reach the overflow from his Earl's Court Crusade as well as audiences assembled in ten outlying cities. The next year, the closed-circuit network was expanded to 27 cities, including tents and theaters in Scotland, Ireland, and Wales. In 1969, the same system will be used for Graham's Madison Square Garden Crusade.

"The response is phenomenal," a Graham aide told me. "In a stadium, you hear his voice and you supply the rest because he's quite a distance away. But on a 20-by-40 foot screen, you achieve the same intimacy you get with a theater telecast of a prizefight. Some of our churchmen said afterwards that, if they were offered a choice between a live appearance by Billy Graham and a closed-circuit telecast, they might be inclined to choose closed-circuit. You're in darkness, your attention is concentrated, and at the end you can come forward to make your decision for Christ by standing in front of the screen. We had twice the response to Mr. Graham's invitation in the closed-circuit auditoriums than we did at Earl's Court." (Ordinarily, according to a BGEA fact sheet, "3.16 per cent of a Crusade audience responds to the invitation 'to be born again.' ")

There are counselors and spiritual advisors on hand at these telecasts, just as there are at theater and church screenings of BGEA's World Wide Films. A favorite is *The Restless Ones,* which has been shown 899 times (usually for $1 admission) in the past 18 months to a total of 3,023,809 people—of whom 200,545 (nearly 7 per cent) came forward to "register decisions for Christ."

The Restless Ones starts in high with a scene of church vandalism and a jangling rock 'n' roll title song:

> Oh restless ones, oh restless ones,
> When will you find release?
> The day you give your life to Him
> Your restless way will cease.

It pretty much ends with a pregnant teen-ager slashing her wrists in a truck-stop rest room, thereby driving her frightened escort over the brink of a long-awaited conversion. Soon thereafter, the screen goes blank and the voice of Billy Graham invites you to come forward.

The Billy Graham Team mixes up its media so ingeniously—preaching from an airplane circling Memphis; conducting services at drive-in theaters for carloads of invalids; lapel mikes, klieg lights, and luminous bumper stickers; chartering trains to distant Crusades and offering group-rate Bible Study Cruises to the Holy Land and the

Billy Graham takes a solitary walk along Isla Verde Beach in San Juan.

Caribbean*—that one can dimly perceive why it has been accused of engineering mass consent. There are even those who claim that Billy Graham himself is a *product* of the media, rather than a master. They point out that his big breakthrough in the 1949 Los Angeles Crusade came when William Randolph Hearst handed down a two-word memo to his city editors: "PUFF GRAHAM."

> *"Another idol we worship today is Sex . . . Manasseh was guilty of immorality. Not just the NORMAL kind of immorality. He erected altars and held vile and obscene orgies around them. The priests would cut themselves, beat themselves, and THEN commit their immorality—the same thing that's happening today in many areas.*
>
> *"We have men who go with women who are not their wives. But the Bible says we should not have lust in our lives. The Bible says there's pleasure in sin for a season. Ohhhh yes, you can go ahead and have a good time—for a season, for a short time. Then something happens. You become satiated, venal, full. You no longer get the same kick and the same ecstasy and the same joy."*

Returning with Billy Graham from a long walk on the beach at San Juan, I spotted an interesting sight ahead: an athletic young couple locked in the deepest throes of passion. As we approached, I was surprised to note that both the girl and her partner still had their bikinis on. Just then, a wrench of lovemaking flipped the sultry Puerto Rican girl onto her back. There she lay, gazing upward, her lips working with silent ecstasy—until her eyes caught sight of Billy Graham, in bathing trunks and sunglasses, advancing upon her like the avenging angel of the beach.

Her mouth froze and her body went limp in her lover's embrace.

While her partner muttered *"Qué pasa?"* and other imprecations, the girl lay still, lifeless, her eyes open wide.

---

* Tour leaders advertised for one jet expedition to the Holy Land were associate evangelist Roy Gustafson and the editor of *Decision* Magazine plus their wives. Another tour included "a visit to Luther Country in East Germany."

Billy Graham nodded to her perfunctorily and went on talking to me about Vietnam.

That night, after Billy Graham had preached on "What Kind of Person Should You Marry?" I stood near the platform watching 429 converts come forward. One was a girl wearing a starched white dress, lace mantilla, and an air of serenity. Her copper skin gleamed in the night lights of Bithorn Stadium. But, if it hadn't been for the wince of recognition she gave when she saw *me*, I might not have recognized her as the girl on the beach.

"Manasseh was guilty of religious pretense. The most scathing denunciations that Jesus ever made were toward the hypocrites, the people who said 'We love thee,' but whose hearts were far from Him; the people who went to the temple and worshipped, but didn't live it during the week; the people who lived to the letter of the law but didn't keep the spirit of the law; the people who would say on the Day of Judgment, 'In Thy name we have built great organizations.' But the seventh chapter of St. Matthew's gospel says: 'And then will I profess unto them, I never knew you: depart from me, ye that work iniquity.' Jesus is going to disown us! For the Bible says —and that's in the Sermon on the Mount!—that 'a good tree cannot bring forth evil fruit, neither can a corrupt tree bring forth good fruits.' "

Flying three abreast from New York to Minneapolis, I found myself sandwiched between two Minneapolitans—a lawyer and a salesman. Over dinner, they asked me why I was visiting their fair city. I told them I was writing about Billy Graham and his organization. "Very interesting, hmmmm?" said the salesman. "But what has Billy Graham got to do with Minneapolis?" "I seem to remember," said the lawyer, "that he used to be president of Northwestern College back in the '40's. Is that it?"

When I told them that their city was Billy Graham's world headquarters and that the Billy Graham Evangelistic Association was the largest user of the U. S. mails in Minneapolis, both men eyed me politely but dubiously—as though reluctant to contradict a religious fanatic.

The next morning, I reported to an unpretentious complex of three red-brick buildings (the highest four stories tall) interconnected by a second-story bridge and a basement tunnel at 13th and Harmon Place in a parish of Minneapolis that ordinarily ministers to automobiles. BGEA's world headquarters, in fact, used to be a garage. No imposing signs or ornate lettering proclaim that this is the hub of a $10-million-a-year global industry; there is just the name "Billy Graham Evangelistic Association" on a glass door. You have to be looking for it to find it.

While there are three tours of the facilities daily for "interested groups," George Wilson, who runs the Minneapolis headquarters, admits that he doesn't encourage publicity about what goes on there. "We're in trouble," he told me, "whenever one of you fellows writes about our computers and our eight-figure-a-year budget. The fellow we depend on—the fellow who sends in five or six dollars—begins to feel mighty small when he reads about this."

Still, total concealment is out of the question with a permanent staff of 450 employees working there.* And, once a visitor gains admission, he can count on his host's pride in ownership and the disarming openness of the Graham organization to lead him into every nook and crevice of this automated wonderland.

George Wilson, a beady-eyed direct-mail genius who has given guest lectures at UCLA and elsewhere on BGEA's computer and scanner techniques, is the best of all possible guides. He calls your attention to the serial number on BGEA's Control Data 915 Page Reader, which is gorging itself on several thousand names and addresses a minute. The serial number is 6 and George Wilson seems surprised that there are five businessmen in this world who automated faster than he did.

In the computer department, he puts a GE 425 computer

---

* Twice a year, when Billy Graham goes on television, his Minneapolis office adds 100 temporary employees to handle the 100,000 extra letters that will pour in during each of those weeks. In 1965, when the Minnesota Twins clinched the American League pennant while Graham was on TV, the mail to BGEA on the first day of World Series ticket sales was greater than the mail to the Twins.

to work for you. In 45 seconds, it calculates and prints the dates of Easter Sunday for every one of 4,500 years—April 2, 500, to April 7, 4999. Working 40 hours a week with pencil, paper, and typewriter, a human being would take at least two months to produce the same table. Then Wilson bends over to demonstrate that every square tile on the computer-room floor is removable—to enable repairmen and technicians to get at the cables underneath.

In the Systems and Procedures Department, a dozen women are processing some of the 100,000 changes of address that come in every month (4,000 to 5,000 of these "changes of address" are "deceased"). Wilson leads you past a stack of tautly-rolled paper—18 inches wide and 10 miles long, he informs you—required for one monthly mailing of *Decision* Magazine.

He also shows you the check-out and check-in offices for BGEA's Home Workers Corps—50 or 60 housewives who take home names-and-addresses and type them up to be fed into the computer on tape. They are paid by an hourly quota. "We used to use punch cards and one girl could do 600 or 700 a day at a machine here," says Wilson. "With tape, a woman working at home can do 1,500 names a day."

Halfway through your tour, George Wilson invites you to take a coffee break with him in the honor-system company cafeteria on the second floor. The cash register is used there only at lunch time. Just off the cafeteria are two chapels—a 65-seat auditorium, Colonial style, where employees can pray during the day, and a 300-seat auditorium, tinselly modern, for formal prayer services and employees' weddings.

You notice that there are hardly any photos or paintings of Billy Graham on the walls and you learn that he quails a little whenever he comes face-to-face with a bigger-than-life blowup of himself. His own paneled office is deserted, except for a lone secretary. The president of the evangelistic association that bears his name seldom visits Minneapolis more than once or twice a year.

On the ground floor is a small Christian Book Shop that does an enormous mail-order business. "When someone writes in for a book by or about Mr. Graham," George Wilson explains, "we don't tell them to write to Doubleday or McGraw-Hill. There are a lot of people who've never heard of Doubleday or McGraw-Hill and wouldn't know how to go about finding them. So we make the books available to them right here at list price." Everything fiscal, in fact, at BGEA is streamlined for customer or contributor convenience. Business-reply envelopes accompanying fund-raising solicitations contain a detachable flap that is a check blank. "THIS IS A CHECK FOR SPREADING THE GOSPEL," it says. You fill in the usual names and amounts plus the name of your local bank and branch without ever having to search for your checkbook. You tear off the check and, as you stuff it in, you notice that the back of the envelope now reads: "With God as my helper, and in dependence upon Him, I make the following pledge: ☐ prayer support. ☐ financial support . . . $...............weekly . . . $............... monthly. . . . All contributions to the Billy Graham Evangelistic Association are income tax deductible."

George Wilson helps you on with your coat and you both walk a couple of blocks to a fourth building, entirely devoted to outgoing mail: "This is an around-the-clock operation, three shifts a day, six days a week. We stop from midnight Saturday to midnight Sunday. I keep threatening Billy that, if our load increases, I'm going to have Seventh Day Adventists in to work that extra day."

Part of the load represents George Wilson's own constant testing and re-evaluating of direct-mail marketing techniques. Which is a better premium to offer with $2-a-year subscriptions to *Decision*—a paperback edition of *World Aflame* (retail value: 75 cents) or a "Billy Graham Verse-A-Day Scripture Key Chain" attached to a miniature Bible containing 31 excerpts (retail value: $1)? George Wilson and his Batch Control Department will know when the results of this month's test mailings are in.

So sophisticated is the BGEA outgoing-mail operation that the U. S. Post Office used it as a pilot study to test the efficiency of the Zip Code system. Nobody will tell what the results are, but George Wilson says Zip Codes won't work properly "until the Post Office brings its computer-and-scanning technology up to our level."

After leaving this building, you double back to the main complex to see how Incoming Mail is processed. Of the million-and-a-half letters a year that pour into Minneapolis, only a small fraction of it has to be forwarded to Graham or one of the branch offices. The bulk of it can be handled right here in Minneapolis.

A first reader opens each envelope and attaches a form chosen according to an elaborate color code: e.g., yellow form=non-donor who needs help; various shades of blue and brown signify donors with problems or questions that require replies; white form = donors with no special requests.

Mail to which white forms are attached is known as "pure mail" and most of these donors are sent letters of acknowledgment within 24 hours. Their names and addresses are typed onto tape, which is then fed into an automatic typewriter that produces one or two personal thank-you notes per minute. Eight of these machines were going full blast when I visited a room staffed by two women who were stuffing them into pre-addressed envelopes. George Wilson changes the acknowledgment message "every week or two."

Rummaging through a first-reader's mail after she had color-coded them, I concentrated on the yellow-formed ones representing strangers in distress asking Billy Graham for free help. One was marked "Home Problem," another "Negro Problem," and still another "Seeking God's will and wanting advice." On each letter, the first readers had underscored its pertinent highlights.

The one I quietly decided to follow up bore a yellow form marked "URGENT!" beneath which the alert first reader had scrawled: "Committed adultery, thinking of suicide." It was a letter from a Louisiana housewife who had gone to bed just once with her next-door neighbor, a man with "a lovely wife and two lovely children," and was now two months pregnant by him.

It was now Wednesday at 10:45 A.M. The letter had been dated Sunday (possibly after the "Hour of Decision") and postmarked Monday. I tossed it back into the reader's outgoing basket without showing any special interest in it.

At 12 noon, however, I asked rather pointedly what had become of that particular letter. George Wilson led me to the Spiritual Counseling Department, where a squad of secretaries were answering the more routine inquiries by stuffing envelopes with pamphlets like "God is for the Alcoholic," prescribing bibliotherapy (books that help), and drafting replies from a "Manual of Suggested Paragraphs" (Paragraph 234: "Child Reared in Christian Home").

The more complicated pleas had been bucked up to the head spiritual counselor, the Rev. John D. Lundberg, and three pastors who assist him full-time. Problems that recur or possess universal interest are excerpted by them and form the basis of "My Answer," Billy Graham's newspaper column.* Publishable answers are drafted here, too, but the final reply is dictated by Graham himself, wherever he is.

The Louisiana lady's letter had landed on Lundberg's desk less than an hour ago. Upon reading it, he had looked up the names of Louisiana pastors in the *Yearbook of American Churches,* found the name of a minister in her community whom he had met and found trustworthy, and phoned him at once. Help was already on the way. A letter from Lundberg would follow later in the day. I had stumbled onto a remarkable spontaneous display of personalized automation in action.

The way George Wilson sees his empire, BGEA has "at least seven ministries" and this is how he ranks them in order of priority:

"Our Crusades. Our radio and TV ministry. Our film ministry. Our magazine ministry. Our counselor training and follow-up. Our Bible Study Correspondence Courses. And these people here who handle the letters with a Bible

---

* Both the title and the column were conceived by the ubiquitous Fred Dienert and Walter Bennett. "My Answer" is syndicated to 146 newspapers by the Chicago *Tribune*-New York *Daily News* organization. Its title was modeled after Eleanor Roosevelt's column, "My Day."

in one hand and the means to find the answers in the other hand.''

BGEA budgets $500,000 a year for those last three ministries; another $500,000 for its film ministry; $4 million for its radio and TV ministry; and $5 million for its magazine ministry. (The Crusades, being locally financed, do not figure as a major budgetary item.)

Decision's 4-million paid subscriptions ($2 a year) barely cover the outlay for the magazine ministry, since there are additional expenses due to rising costs and the investment in a free one-year subscription awarded to each convert who registers a decision for Christ at a Graham event. (Also published under Graham auspices, but in Washington, is *Christianity Today,* with a paid circulation of 150,000, largely ministers.)

Decision looks like a Sunday supplement with no paid advertising. It usually leads off with a front-page article by Billy Graham. The May, 1967, issue was 16 pages. It featured a cover photo of Billy Graham's mother above an essay on how to keep your house in order, written by her illustrious son. Inside were: an editorial wholeheartedly advocating courtesy . . . ''Gumdrops and Peppermints,'' a nostalgic reminiscence about the Christian influence of the oldtime candy store . . . excerpts from several religious books . . . a two-page center spread on a recent Crusade, written by editor Sherwood Eliot Wirt . . . a Datebook of Associate Evangelist schedules, impending engagements for World Wide pictures, and previews of coming Crusades . . . ''Christ at Expo 67'' . . . and my own favorite, ''Rug Cleaning with God,'' an autobiographical article by a businessman named Marion E. Wade. It was subtitled ''A man in the business of killing moths finds God setting him up in a new business—His.''

Founded in 1960 and now published bi-monthly in French, German, and Spanish editions (circulation: 50,000 each), *Decision* embodies a publishing success story rivaled only by *Playboy*. Since both *Playboy* and *Decision* were passing the 4-million circulation mark within a few months of each other, I made this comparison to George Wilson. He appeared to be complimented, even though he snapped:

"Don't ever mention *that* in the same breath."

George Wilson is a go-getter who keeps *The Wall Street Journal* alongside the Bible on his desk. His new car is equipped to play taped organ music in stereo on his way to and from work. He describes his job—and BGEA's for that matter—as "to dispense the world's greatest product with the greatest economy to the greatest number of people as fast as possible." *Decision* was his brain child and so was the Billy Graham Pavilion, BGEA's toweringly gold-tipped erection at the 1964-65 New York World's Fair. It was the first and tallest sight to greet you as you came off the subway or parked your car.

When George first broached the idea at a BGEA Board of Directors meeting in late 1962, he ran into some opposition because nobody knew what the costs and fees would be. To look into it further, George hopped the next morning's plane to New York and went directly from Idlewild Airport to the Fair's Flushing Meadow site. At that early date, the Fair consisted of mud, dust, debris, and an administration building. There, Wilson asked to see the Fair's director.

The New York World's Fair's tallest tower was Billy Graham's.

BG

"Do you have an appointment with Mr. [Robert] Moses?" a secretary asked him.

"No," said George, who confesses now that he "didn't know Moses from Adam's off-ox." After half-an-hour, he was ushered into Moses' presence.

"What do you want to do, young man?" Robert Moses asked him.

"I'm looking for a place to show our movies," said George Wilson.

"You want a building then," said Moses.

"Not if we can just rent space in some other building," said George.

"Can't be done," said Moses. "By the way, who do you represent?"

"Billy Graham," said George, taking a deep breath.

After a lengthy moment of meditation, Moses said: "I'll tell you what, Wilson. I *know* Billy Graham. And since we're giving one building to the Vatican, one building to the Mormons, and so on and so forth—and Billy Graham's as big as any of them—why don't we give *him* some space, too?"

Moses pressed a couple of buzzers and then started to reel off a list of sites the Fair would be willing to donate.

"If you don't mind, sir," George interrupted, "I'd just as soon have whichever is nearest to the main gate."

Moses gave him 72,000 square feet just inside the main gate and sent him to see "an architect fellow he knew named Edward Durrell Stone. Moses told Stone to waive his fee." Stone designed a 100-foot tower with airy loggias, panels of color transparencies, and a 350-seat theater for showing World Wide's Todd-AO production of *Man in the Fifth Dimension*. The Pavilion's first convert was the Todd-AO representative.

Stone, says George Wilson, envisioned "a little jewel of a pavilion, but I kept bugging him and the others about getting it up in the air and putting lights on it." Before Wilson and Stone and Moses were done, the Billy Graham Pavilion thrust 117 feet high ("nine feet taller than anything else there and a little higher than anything was allowed to be," says Wilson) and glittered with 4,000 gold-anodized discs. Hourly screenings of *Man in the Fifth Dimension* helped to attract a two-year total of 5-million visitors, with a steady stream of converts coming forward. But Billy Graham had to curtail a World's Fair visit with his family a few minutes after venturing out of the Billy Graham Pavilion. A friendly mob of fairgoers spotted him, jostled to see him, and thus all he saw was them.

George Wilson is not only BGEA's top Organization Man, but he is also the prototype of the others I met in Minneapolis and on subsequent visits to the Atlanta and London offices. On first meeting, the Team members seemed every bit as loyal but interchangeable as their IBM and GE counterparts I knew back east. But after I'd known the BGEA people for a few minutes, I perceived that—unlike all other Organization Men I knew—they had required no on-the-job indoctrination to truly believe in the work they were doing.

> *"Manasseh was a murderer. Now he was no ordinary murderer. He was a sadistic murderer. Thousands of people slaughtered for no reason at all—just at his whims. The Bible says in Second Kings 21:16: 'Moreover Manasseh shed innocent blood very much, till he had filled Jerusalem from one end to another . . .' Think of it! He filled Jerusalem with blood from one end to the other. What a wicked, vile man!"*

Early in 1966, President Johnson was showing Billy Graham around the LBJ Ranch in Texas. The President was driving, but he suddenly stopped the car, looked at his passenger, and said: "When are you going to Vietnam?"

Billy Graham replied: "Mr. President, I'll try to go at Christmas."

The President said: "Well, that's quite a long time [but] all right. You tell me exactly when you want to go. *We* want you to go. I want you to go out there and talk to those men and learn all you can about the situation out there." *

---

* This dialogue is taken from Billy Graham's own recollections of his conversation with the President.

A while later, Graham received a formal invitation from the American military commander in Vietnam, General William C. Westmoreland. And so, in December, 1966 it came to pass that Billy Graham flew to Vietnam to tell the troops that "the peace Jesus Christ brought on the first Christmas can give you peace even in the midst of war."

At the Third Field Hospital in Saigon, he visited a man who had been "all shot to pieces." They didn't know whether he would live or die. But he told me, 'I have peace.' " Later, Graham told a gathering of American, Australian, and New Zealand airmen: "That man had the peace of God and you can have it, too. God comes into your heart and gives you that peace."

He ministered to "men in hospitals with arms shot off and legs shot off. I saw a man with shrapnel in his brain. The doctors said he didn't understand. He didn't know where *he* was. He didn't know who *I* was. I said a prayer. He gripped my hand with his hand. And then he whispered 'Merry Christmas.' I had to turn away so he wouldn't see the tears in my eyes."

In jet-powered helicopters, he traveled to isolated outposts—flying high because "the Viet Cong are pretty accurate with their guns at 3,000 feet. Then we'd communicate by radio that we were coming and they'd send up a yellow sulphur flare and we'd drop right down there. There'd be six Marines and they'd have 25 Vietnamese troops with them. And we'd have a little five-minute Christmas service and then take off. You could visit three or four of these outposts in an hour."

Other troops were flown to hear him. A Marine captain wrote home to his wife:

> Nancy dearest:
> I've been swimming in the Lord all day and just can't stop . . . I got a chance to fly to Da Nang this morning and I went and saw and heard Billy Graham. Nancy, he is tremendous, really. In person he is more powerful than he seems on TV or radio; that guy just breathes Jesus Christ.

At Long Binh, three days before Christmas, Billy Graham told 5,000 GIs that "millions of Americans are very proud

He preaches at Danang Marine Base, Christmas, 1966.

of you. Their prayers and hopes are with you. God bless you.''

He also told them about a man who went hunting for bear without a weapon:

''After half an hour, he came running back toward a cabin where his two friends were. They heard him hollering 'Open that door! Open that door!' They looked out and saw a big bear chasing him. They opened the door, but just before he got there, the man stepped aside and the bear ran in. The man shut the door and shouted through the window, 'Skin that one, and I'll go get another one.' ''

The audience chuckled.

Then Graham added: ''You might work that on Charlie sometime.''

The audience roared with glee. Charlie was the Viet Cong.

Graham's eight-day tour of Vietnam did not go unnoticed in the world press, although another visitor to Vietnam generated the headlines: "CARDINAL SPELLMAN PROCLAIMS VIETNAM STRUGGLE 'HOLY WAR.'" Bob Hope was there, too, and he wrote a syndicated column about Billy Graham: "Meeting him makes it easy to understand why people of all faiths respond so warmly to this dynamic spiritual leader. Billy really moves a crowd." Hope then added, erroneously: "Fortunately, he doesn't get laughs."

In March of 1967, a couple of weeks before Billy Graham came to Puerto Rico, *Time* Magazine listed an earlier Latin American tour of his among the beneficiaries of U. S. Central Intelligence Agency funds. Before this particular scandal had run its course, almost everything respectable—from *Encounter* Magazine to the Harvard Law School Fund—was "unmasked" in the press as a CIA front. But, at the time Billy Graham's plane touched down at San Juan International Airport, the newspapers of Puerto Rico were printing letters-to-the-editors denouncing this alleged link between Church and State as "anathema" and "unconstitutional."

A BGEA advance man had already said "so far as we know, CIA has never given us a penny since we started—unless some CIA man dropped a penny into the offering plate." But, at his first press conference in San Juan, Billy Graham unwittingly strengthened his quasi-official status by announcing that "we are on the verge of seeing some startling developments in Vietnam." He hinted that the United States might be negotiating a peace agreement and then cut off the discussion of international affairs with: "I can't go any further than that. No, I haven't been in Washington, but I have been on the phone quite often."

It was eight days before a statement from Graham on CIA financing broke into print: "I would never accept funds from any Government agency. I wouldn't even take a loan. And certainly not from the CIA. That would be dynamite. I strongly believe in the separation between Church and State. The story in *Time* Magazine was the first I'd ever heard about CIA financing a Crusade. We have never received any funding that we know about. The money might have come through some other organization." He promised to investigate the matter upon his return to the mainland.

The day before, the English-language San Juan *Star* had printed this letter from an Associate Professor of political science at the University of Puerto Rico:

"A great deal of fanfare and Madison Avenue type publicity has preceded the arrival to our island of evangelist Billy Graham, prominent together with Cardinal Spellman among the more strident hawks in the Vietnamese war. The primitive fundamentalism of Mr. Graham, together with his scarcely disguised jingoism of the 'our country right or wrong' variety makes a mockery of the original Christian message, a message based upon love and forgiveness for all peoples and not upon a narrow, chauvinistic, Messianic conception of a chosen people out to 'civilize' mankind through germ warfare, napalm, and saturation bombing.

". . . Mr. Graham visited Vietnam and he was scarcely below par with Cardinal Spellman in his all out endorsement of the 'holy' war that the United States wages against the Vietnamese people. His homely example about the man who went out bear hunting without a weapon ended with a statement 'working it on Charlie the Viet Cong—sometime.' As a matter of fact, Mr. Graham has fully endorsed the notion that 'Charlie' is of a different species from GI Joe, an oriental thing, a 'gook,' a less than human creature that can be exterminated as a service to the preservation of 'Christian' civilization.

"It is no wonder if according to . . . *Time* magazine the CIA partly financed Mr. Graham's tour through Latin America. The top espionage agency of the North American empire can lie back and be sure that Mr. Graham's message will be fully in accordance with the stated aims of American foreign policy in Latin America and in the rest of the world. His blessing will always be available for all those that endlessly pursue the task of oppressing or attempting to oppress the people that comprise more than two-thirds of the world population."

Clearly, the professor had read much more into the news accounts than the rest of us might have. And, to one who had observed Billy Graham for all of a week when the letter appeared, it didn't jibe with the man I was getting to know. Nevertheless, there were details in the whole chronology of events that troubled me. I clipped the letter for future clarification by Billy Graham.

"Tradition tells us that Manasseh had Isaiah the prophet sawed in two. You say, 'If ever a man deserved hell, that man deserved hell.' He took his own child and burned

him. He took little innocent babies from their mothers and sacrificed them to the great god Moloch. Manasseh—the most wicked, vile man."

We were sitting on the sands of Isla Verde Beach when I reached into my beach robe and handed Billy Graham the professor's letter. The invective in it didn't seem to faze him at all.

"I told the story about the man and the bear," he said, handing the letter back to me, "to make the guys laugh a little. I wanted to show them I was not a Holy Joe."

"And what about telling them they might try it on Charlie some time?"

"If you want to be technical about it," Graham said, "that's a pacifist joke. The man went out without a gun to get the bear."

"Are you a pacifist?"

"I'm not a pacifist in any situation. I'm for peace. I believe in peace. I've said that the military aspect of the war is in the hands of the President and the military men, who know far more about it than any clergyman in the pulpit. I told President Johnson before I went that I wasn't entering the hawk or dove side of the war. I've not even taken a position on whether we should be in Vietnam. And the President said, 'All right, Billy. When those newspaper guys get you in a corner, just tell them you're a friend of the President of the United States and he'll go anywhere in the world for peace.' "

I waited for Graham to go on. When he didn't, I asked if his conduct in Vietnam might not have lent a religious endorsement to one side of a war that both sides quite righteously believe in.

"My ministry is a world-wide ministry," Graham replied. "I went there to minister to the men. I told them 'it's a courageous thing you're doing.' There are heroes . . ." His voice trailed off and then came back strong. "You know, elsewhere in the Far East I find that people have tremendous respect for America *because* of our presence in Vietnam. But back home, the doves have criticized me for

Billy Graham and the author hold informal interview.

going there and the hawks have criticized me for not taking a stand. But my skin is two yards thick.''

I asked Billy Graham how an airman, for example, could accept what Graham preached and then—even under orders!—go on a mission that would inevitably sear, mutilate, and destroy children, the most innocent of bystanders?

"The development of the napalm bomb," he replied, "was by the British, you know. It was first used in the bombing of Hamburg. Those two nights over Hamburg with napalm destroyed more people than the atom bomb did in Nagasaki. People came out of houses with their bodies on fire and ran screaming into the lake . . .''

I interrupted him to say: "If you preached in Vietnam some of the same messages you preached here . . .''

"I certainly did," he said crisply.

"And if a comparable number of people came forward and made decisions for Christ . . .''

"I never ask them to come forward," Graham interjected. "On military bases and at state universities, I respect my obligation not to proselytize.''

"Even so," I said. "If you preached your message and it came across there the way it does here, I'm surprised I didn't read in the next day's paper about wholesale desertions from General Westmoreland's army."

Billy Graham blazed back: "There is nothing in the Bible that says you shouldn't be a soldier. King David was a soldier and he was called the Friend of God. Abraham destroyed whole towns when he went to rescue Lot." Citing more chapter-and-verse, he noted that the Viet Cong's victims have "eyes gouged out and testicles cut off." Only then did his voice soften. "War is a tragedy," he went on. "We should do everything in our power to avoid it. I couldn't do it personally. War is a terrible sin—a sin against all humanity. But the people who fight war are no more wicked than the rest of us. Their work can be very unpleasant. So can police work."

At this point, I dropped the subject. But Billy Graham wasn't quite finished kicking it around:

"Man is a fighting animal. Man is a diseased animal. But the Bible says there is a coming day of peace. The Bible says we must pray for peace. We are commanded in the Bible to pray for peace. Every morning I get up and pray for peace. But the peace we pray for must have a definition. Is it a peace of surrender? I would not have settled for peace as long as Hitler was overrunning Europe. When I was invited to preach in Berlin, I said I could not come without speaking to the Jewish world and asking forgiveness for the Christian church. And I did . . ."

"You'll probably find me evasive on Vietnam. I don't want to take a stand. I'm not in a position to tell President Johnson how to run the war. He would do anything to get out of the Vietnam war. He really wanted to change our country, but he's gotten bogged in the Vietnam war. There will be an end. I've been with the President long enough to know that this is the only man who has the answer."

We walked back to the Holiday Inn and had lunch.*

---

* Nowadays, Billy Graham's diet during Crusades is as follows: Breakfast of two eggs and bacon with hot tea. A lunch similar to the one described on the next page. A grilled cheese sandwich and a cup of hot tea before preaching and "nothing else afterwards except maybe a root beer."

Graham ordered a hamburger and iced tea. When the iced tea came, he remarked: "When I got married, one of the first things I told Ruth was, 'You have a standing order for iced tea every day.' "

He sipped the tea, nodded approval, and then went on: "I'm told that reformed alcoholics live on this stuff. It meets their immediate thirst and keeps them out of trouble."

I told Graham of a reformed alcoholic I'd interviewed who kept a vase of iced tea on his desk to alleviate stress. Whenever I'd ask a difficult question, his face would practically disappear into the vase and wouldn't emerge until the tea was drained or his answer was ready.

"I know what you mean," said Graham. "If I'd had some iced tea when we were back on the beach, I could have jumped into it when you were questioning me about Vietnam."

"You say, 'But we're not murderers!' You've never killed anybody with a knife or gun. But your thoughts have murdered them. The Bible talks about smiting with our tongues. You can kill another's reputation with an ugly story that you tell. Christ says the fulfillment of all the law and the prophets was love—love for God and love for our fellow man. The Scripture says in First Corinthians 13:5, 'Love thinketh no evil.' ... If you have love, you are not only going to think no evil, you're going to take your tongue and have it nailed to the cross so that you bless instead of curse."

Billy Graham does not disapprove of smoking or drinking—by others. He once told Harold H. Martin of *The Saturday Evening Post*: "What may be sin to me may not be sin to you. I don't smoke or drink because I look upon the human body as God's temple which should be kept pure and strong and healthy for His service."

In Puerto Rico, Billy Graham took most of his meals in his room. But, whenever a member of his Team joined my family at the dinner table, my wife and I couldn't help noticing that he seemed disturbed if we were having cocktails. If, in serving the food, the waiter moved a martini toward the Team man, he would move his chair away from it. Until

Graham is always gallant with female admirers.

the martini glasses were cleared away, he would be ill at ease.

We realized that it was not temptation, but a matter of what the passing public might think upon seeing a Billy Graham Team member with a drink in front of him.

As soon as this dawned upon us, we switched to Bloody Marys—on the assumption that only the evil-minded would presume the most active ingredient. This emphasis on appearances worked, for the most part. But there was one awful moment when—with much of the Team at a nearby table—our daughters set up a clamor of "we want Bloody Marys, too!" Quickly, I whispered to the waiter, "Bring us two more—*without* vodka." The waiter nodded and then, in a voice that electrified the dining room, called to the bartender: "Two Bloody Marys and two Virgin Marys!"

(One of the banes of Billy Graham's "image" is the occasional look-alike who is seen imbibing. A Texas school superintendent named Newell Odell, who is often mistaken for Billy Graham, recently was "recognized" by a waitress who was pouring wine for him. She dropped the bottle. Once, visiting New York at the time of the Madison Square Garden Crusade, Odell went to a café with a woman who resembled Margaret Truman. In the next edition, a gossip column "item" was born.)

The one lunch I had with Billy Graham in the Holiday Inn's outdoor dining room taught me why he takes his meals in his room. Our table became a target of a constant assault by nice, polite, well-meaning tourists who wanted Graham's autograph, handshake, advice, or recollection of a visit to their home town. At the end of the meal, I could scarcely remember eating. But I still recall Graham's hasty and humble interjection as I picked up my fork: "Can we have a prayer first?"

Wherever Billy Graham goes, if there's a Holiday Inn, he and his Team stay there. He was the first VIP ever to receive a Special Holiday Inn Recognition Card that reads: "TO ALL INNKEEPERS. This card entitles BILLY GRAHAM, WORLD EVANGELIST to FREE LODGING at any and all HOLIDAY INNS anywhere at any time.

NON-TRANSFERABLE, NON-EXPIRING.'' The same courtesy is extended to his family; members of his entourage pay half the going rate.

A similar arrangement prevails with the Sheraton Hotel chain around the world, which may be why a wealthy Briton pledged $14,000 toward the 1966 Billy Graham Crusade in London *if* the evangelist would not stay at a big American hotel. Having already arranged to billet Billy Graham at the Kensington Palace—a luxurious, but not super de luxe, British-owned hotel opposite Hyde Park—BGEA cheerfully accepted the condition.

Every night in San Juan my wife and I rode out to Bithorn Stadium in a car or Volkswagen with a number of Team members. In the hotel parking lot, the first person to show up carrying a raincoat was greeted with gleeful whoops of ''Little faith!''

The only kidding with deeper overtones involved Associate Evangelist Ralph Bell, a Negro pastor from Los Angeles whose beat now includes Africa, and Gil A. Stricklin, the Team's very Southern White Anglo-Saxon Protestant press representative. Gil, who works out of Atlanta, is to Graham what Bill Moyers was to Lyndon Johnson—and, as a matter of fact, both Stricklin and Moyers attended Southwestern Baptist Theological Seminary at the same time.

Gil Stricklin is perhaps the most unbigoted Southerner (not to mention the most helpful press agent) I've ever met. But one night in the car he made a Southern Liberal Freudian slip of the tongue. At a traffic light on our way to the Crusade, six dark young beggar boys began polishing our windshield and rapping on our windows for money. The car was airconditioned, so the windows were up. But Gil rolled his down and handed them a nickel to fight over.

''I can't pass them by,'' he explained to Ralph Bell, seated beside him, ''because I always think that there, but for a few breaks in life, goes *you*.''

I could see the back of Ralph's neck bristle as he said: ''What do you mean—*me*?''

''Aw, Ralph,'' said Gil, ''you *know* where I stand on that. I meant *myself*.''

A few nights later, on the way back from a Crusade, Gil Stricklin used in conversation the phrase *"black as sin."*

"Haven't you heard?" Ralph Bell said. "Sin is scarlet this year."

Gil Stricklin sighed, put his arm around Ralph's shoulder, and said with beautiful directness that made Ralph and everybody else laugh: "Ralph Bell. My brother. My friend."

Press aide Gil Stricklin likes to stay highly mobile.

"Every person here tonight is guilty of violating one of the Ten Commandments. And this brings us to race prejudice . . . What was the color of Jesus' skin? Jesus wasn't born white. He was born with a healthy tan and he'd have to show a birth certificate to get into one of your country clubs today."

Billy Graham's Tarheel origins tend to make Jesus Christ sound like a cracker ("Ah are He!"). But this only adds to the message of racial equality he has consistently preached and practiced. "As a Southerner," he says, "I may have a little more influence than a man with a New England accent."

In 1953, fourteen months before the Supreme Court's landmark decision against school segregation, Billy Graham held a deliberately integrated Crusade in Chattanooga. In other Southern cities, when he was told that Jim Crow was the law, he insisted that Negroes be assigned a shaded section of choice seats rather than the usual back bleachers. And, in his invitations, he would urge all races to come forward together: "White and colored alike. Standing before the cross of Christ. There is no racial distinction here. The ground is level at the foot of the cross."

When the Supreme Court decision came, Graham immediately used it as a wedge to integrate his Nashville and New Orleans audiences. All subsequent Crusades have been integrated, too.

In Richmond in 1956, a church member who had volunteered to usher turned in his armband when he was ordered to seat Negroes with whites. "To hell with your revival!" he said. But, within a week, he made a new commitment to Christ and applied for his job back.

In Charlotte in 1958, a white aristocratic lady came forward and was counseled by a Negro woman. When a friend who was with her expressed surprise at her tolerating this, the convert was even more surprised. "Why? Was she a Negro? I hadn't even noticed."

Graham has changed his schedules to preach equality in Little Rock, Birmingham, and Clinton, Tenn., at times of racial turbulence there. He has even converted white su-

Ralph Bell: "Haven't you heard? Sin is scarlet this year."

premacists who came to his meetings with the avowed intention of wrecking them. On the other hand, in 1960, he turned down an invitation from the churches of South Africa "because of the race problem . . . We feel it will be a greater sermon to them leaving South Africa from our itinerary." That same year, in *Reader's Digest,* he lashed out hard at the church back home in an article called "Why Don't the Churches Practice the Brotherhood They Preach?" There—and again to *Time* in 1965—he remarked, as he remarks often, that "the most segregated hour of the week is 11 o'clock Sunday morning."

> *"Manasseh was guilty of all these sins. He was also a traitor. He betrayed every trust he ever had. Many of us betray Christ—for a passionate moment, for an extra dollar, for a little extra recognition, for a better job. Oh yes, we'll betray Christ.*
>
> *"The Bible says that Manasseh went beyond the sins of other nations that God had to blot out. He seemed to have an unholy ambition to excel in wickedness. He became an expert in iniquity, racketeering, gangsterism, prostitution, EVERYTHING!*
>
> *"But watch out, Manasseh! The Bible has said, God has said, 'Be sure your sin will find you out. God will let you get by with it for a while. You can go on for five years, ten years, twenty years, thirty years, and you seem to be beating the game, Manasseh. You can continue, but somewhere, some day, it's gonna catch up with you. Your whole world crashes around you and you have no resources to face it!' If you can commit one sin and get away with it, I would be glad to quit preaching, throw the Bible away, and agree with you that it is not true. But God has said in His holy Word, 'Be sure your sin will find you out.' God also warns, 'Whatsoever a man soweth, that shall he also reap.' You can sow to the wind, but the Bible says, 'Some day you will reap a whirlwind.'"*

Among the case histories that Billy Graham likes to cite in his more recent sermons is "a man who lived in Europe a hundred years ago whose name was Frederick Nietzsche. He was the son of a Lutheran clergyman, but he began to turn against God at the university. He became The Greatest Atheist of his Day! One hundred years ago, Nietzsche wrote a parable in which he had a madman going around with a lantern in the daytime, saying 'God is dead.' That's the first time the expression 'God is dead' was ever used, as far as I know.

"Now Nietzsche was a deep thinker and when Nietzsche said 'God is dead' a hundred years ago, it was a terrible thought to him. It was a tragedy to him. He wrote about the Superman and that's where Hitler got his ideas. But Nietzsche couldn't find happiness. The last twelve years of his life he spent in a mental institution. But now, in our generation, some men—even some churchmen—have pronounced 'God is dead' and they're jumping up and down on His grave that they dug and shouting, 'Hallelujah! God is dead!'"

When I visited Billy Graham's hotel room, I was surprised to find him reading a biography of Nietzsche. I was even more surprised when he confessed that "I've been on this Nietzsche jag for six months—reading everything I can lay hands on by and about him."

At least half of Graham's "studying time"—which averages six to eight hours a day at home and three to four away from home—is devoted to Nietzsche nowadays; the rest is allocated to current events inside and outside the church:

"It was the 'God is dead' controversy that got me interested in the coldness of life without God and so I've been studying Nietzsche ever since. Of course, I go off on tangents —that's part of the joy of studying. I began to realize how much Nietzsche owed to Hegel, so I studied Hegel. Hegel owed so much to Rousseau that I read Rousseau. Right now, I'm looking into the relationship between Karl Marx and Nietzsche—two of the men who've had the greatest influence on the world today. And both were exposed to religion in their youth. In fact, Karl Marx was once reputed to have said 'Jesus Christ was the best man that ever lived.' "

Billy Graham then quoted Karl Marx on God as "the keystone of a perverted society" and concluded with a wistful lament that "if I had my life to live over again, I'd have gone much farther in school."

His fundamentalist schooling and lack of a solid secular education worried Billy Graham during the great intellectual-spiritual crisis of his adult years—which he resolved while he was still president of Northwestern College.

Chuck Templeton, a Youth for Christ associate who had resigned his pastorate to study advanced theology at

Princeton, began to experience what his friend Billy Graham described as "a change of heart toward the Scriptures . . . and now he came to doubt the divine authority of the Bible. My own mind became somewhat unsettled as a result of his arguments . . . Suddenly, I wondered if the Bible could be trusted completely . . . The struggle would last for the next six months."

Graham never doubted the deity of Christ or the Gospel he was preaching, but he was genuinely troubled by Templeton's challenging of his sources and nagging assertions that "your faith is too simple, Billy." When crowds were sparse and apathetic at a ten-day campaign that Graham held in Altoona, Pa., in June of 1949 ("If ever I conducted a flop, that was it"), Graham blamed his own uncertainty. He contemplated leaving evangelism, and knew that he "could not go on if the issue wasn't settled soon."

Then, a couple of weeks before the famous Los Angeles Crusade that September, he went for a walk in the pine-scented San Bernardino Mountains. He prayed as he walked and then he "got to a stump and put my Bible on the stump, and I knelt down, and I said: 'O God, there are many things in this Book I do not understand. But, God, I am going to accept this Book as Your Word by *faith*. I'm going to allow my faith to go beyond my intellect and believe that this is Thy inspired word.' "

"So judgment did fall, not only upon Manasseh, but upon all of Jerusalem. God said, 'I will wipe Jerusalem as a man wipeth a dish, wiping it, and turning it upside down.' He allowed the enemy from the north to move in upon Jerusalem. . . . Manasseh, the great king who sat upon his great golden throne, was pulled off his throne and dragged through the streets by the nose. They put a ring through his nose like an animal, and led him through the streets, and the people spat on him. 'You deserve it,' they said. 'Take that! Take that!' Can't you imagine the stones and the eggs and the spittle and the yelling and the sneering and the obscenities that were flung at him? They HATED him! And if ever a man deserved judgment in death, it was Manasseh."

'We never know when our moment will come . . ."

Billy Graham preaches a gospel of comeuppance with awesome fundamentalist fervor: "It seems that the demons of hell have been let loose. The fires of passion, hate, greed, and lust are sweeping over the world and we seem to be plunging toward Armageddon. This is the tormented generation. This is the generation destined to live in the midst of crisis, fear, and death. We are like a people under the sentence of death, waiting for the date of execution to be set. We sense that something is about to happen. We know that things cannot go on as they are. History seems to have reached an impasse. We are on a collision course. Something is about to give, and all of mankind is crying tonight, 'What must I do to be saved?' "

Often, he sketches this retribution in modern idiom:

"How many of you have Social Security? Hospitalization? Insurance? All is in order in your lives! But you may drop dead tomorrow!

"A judge sat in a Senator's office and waited all morning. When the Senator came out, the judge said, 'Senator, may I see you for one minute?' And the Senator said, 'If Jesus Christ asked me for one minute of, time this morning, I couldn't give it to Him.' Then he walked out of the office and dropped dead on the steps of the Senate.

"This was the sin of Sodom; it is the sin of many who are here tonight. You don't pray much. You don't read your Bible. You don't live for Christ! And you don't have time for God! . . .

"On Christmas Eve, Cliff Barrows and I were high in the mountains of Vietnam. Sitting in the audience was a handsome young general. I had just had dinner with him. That was last Christmas Eve. In today's newspaper, that young general is said to have dropped dead of a heart attack. We never know when our moment will come . . ."

In the same vein, he tells of a man talking to his minister: "Oh, I know I've got to get right with God. But I'm too busy now. I'll do it on my death bed, when I have time." Then Graham reminds his listeners that "in our last hours and the way they drug you today, you may not have a chance to repent even if you want to. You'd better come now, while you can."

Graham answers cautiously to the label of "fundamentalist." He wrote in *Look* in 1956:

"There are so many shades of fundamentalism and so many shades of liberalism, it is increasingly difficult to point to a man and say he is a 'liberal' or he is a 'fundamentalist' without qualifying explanation. If by *fundamentalist* you mean 'narrow,' 'bigoted,' 'prejudiced,' 'extremist,' 'emotional, 'snake-handler,' 'without social conscience'—then I am definitely not a fundamentalist. However, if by *fundamentalist* you mean a person who accepts the authority of the Scriptures, the virgin birth of Christ, the atoning death of Christ, His bodily resurrection, His second coming, and personal salvation by faith through grace, then I am a fundamentalist. However, I much prefer being called a 'Christian.' "

Graham also considers himself a "liberal." Discussing

the U. S. Senate's earliest Republican "dove," Graham remarked to me on the beach at San Juan: "Mark Hatfield's theology and mine are identical. We're both liberals and yet we differ on Vietnam."

Still, closing your eyes, you can almost imagine you're hearing Dwight L. Moody or Mordecai Ham or William Jennings Bryan even while Billy Graham punctuates the time-honored language of evangelism with the heresies of Darwin and Galileo:

"The greatest problem in the world today is the increase in population. The number of people in the world will double in the next few years. Knowledge will also double. Your children will have to learn twice as much as you know. The world is changing. Perhaps the biggest changes will be taking place right here in Latin America. Political change. Social change. Scientific change. But some things never change. The Bible says that some things can never be changed. The sun comes up. The world turns round. And if it varies even slightly, we will all be killed."

He pauses to permit a Pan Am jet to scream past and then, before its thunder has ceased to rumble, Billy Graham booms out:

"AND GOD NEVER NEVER NEVER NEVER NEVER EVER CHANGES!

"And the Bible says: 'I AM THE LORD. I CHANGE NOT.'"

Six weeks later, in Montreat, when I told Billy Graham I'd chosen his sermon on "The Wickedest Man Who Ever Lived" as my literary framework for writing about him, he expressed pleasure: "I'm glad you picked out that one. I give it often because human beings never change. You put a little chrome and silver on someone and you still have a human being. There was lying and killing in the Bible. We have more education today. We've improved men's minds, but you study the Bible and you study the morning newspaper and you see that they carry the same stories. Manasseh was the Hitler of his day."

Then Graham turned to me and asked point-blank: "Would *you* have forgiven Hitler?"

"They carried Manasseh 1,500 miles away to Babylon and put him in a cold, damp dungeon, and you say, 'He deserved it.' If that had happened here, if he had slain your children and had torn down all your churches, and taken your Bible and burned it, if he had done that, you too might have been in the crowd that spat upon him and hated him and said that he deserved to be executed.

"BUT WAIT A MINUTE! You don't yet understand the mercy of God! God is a God of justice, but He is also a God of mercy. While Manasseh was in that dungeon he began to realize the wicked things he had done. His conscience began to speak to him. God's Holy Spirit began to work upon his soul. So it is with us.

"Many times the events that seem tragic in life are allowed by God in order to speak to us. You see, the Bible says that the goodness of God should lead us to repentance. God has been good to us. The very goodness of God should drive us to Jesus Christ. But, instead of driving us toward Christ, it seems to have driven us away from Christ. We have followed the materialism of our times and maybe—MAYBE—God may allow judgment to come in order to drive us to the cross in repentance to plead for forgiveness.

"Manasseh was in prison and he was praying for repentance, and he said, 'GOD, FORGIVE ME, FORGIVE ME, FORGIVE ME, FORGIVE ME!'"

"What would you have done? If you were God, would you have forgiven him? He didn't do anything to earn forgiveness. All he did was to say, 'God, I'm sorry. Forgive me. If you'll give me another chance, O God, I'll follow you and serve you and live for you. O God, I've made a tragic mistake. I've sinned. Will you please forgive me?'

"If you were God what would you do? . . ."

Having described Billy Graham earlier as the one evangelist who can go nine innings with relative ease, I might add that he could just as easily go seventeen. For he is the untiring master of his art. He can fire in those blazing repetitions—"GOD NEVER NEVER NEVER NEVER EVER CHANGES" and "GOD, FORGIVE ME, FORGIVE

ME, FORGIVE ME, FORGIVE ME''—whenever he needs
a third strike. Or he can mix up his stuff and weave a subtle
web of tantalizing curves and hooks that all hang in there
with one perfect sermon—45 minutes spent raveling and
unraveling the riddle of what Jesus meant when he said
three words, ''Remember Lot's wife.''

Another of Billy Graham's gifts is virtuoso storytelling.
In his best sermons like ''The Wickedest Man Who Ever
Lived,'' he tells a tale on two levels simultaneously—the
Biblical for narrative and the contemporary for meaning
—with the utmost purity, sincerity, and polish. While the
version herein of ''Wickedest Man'' is drastically condensed, there is enough of it to demonstrate the high-dra-
matic drive with which the 1969-model Billy Graham shifts
from one level of spellbinding to another, varying only the
intensity. For there is no man talking or writing in America
today who can make story and moral mesh so inevitably and
yet so invisibly as Billy Graham does.

Graham could also hold his own with Bob Hope at his best
as a stand-up humorist. One of the stories he tells most
often on the platform is about ''the fattest man I ever saw.
He was getting into an airplane I was taking and they had
to remove the arm rest and squeeze him into two seats. He
was drunk. He was cursing. He was swearing. He was trying
to flirt with the stewardess. Nobody liked him. Finally, the
plane got up into the air. He was out of his seat. 'I'm gonna
help the pilot fly the plane!' he said. Everybody got nervous.
The co-pilot came out and helped both stewardesses sit him
down. He started cursing and swearing again. Then someone
tried to keep him quiet by telling him I was sitting behind
him. He was up out of his seat. 'Are you Billy Graham? I
want to shake your hand. Your sermons have helped me so
very much!'''

Graham told me a similar story about Dwight L. Moody,
the evangelist whose method of invitation he says he ''copies the hardest.'' Moody's attention once was directed to a
staggering drunk on the verge of passing out: ''Mr. Moody,
there goes one of your converts.'' To which Moody replied:

"Tell your wife you love her, but don't let her faint."

Everywhere Graham goes, the big questions follow

"Well, it must be one of mine because it certainly isn't one of the Lord's."

On the "Tonight" show in 1967, Graham discussed a telegram of advice and encouragement he had received from someone who signed himself "The Christ." Graham quipped to Johnny Carson that "I don't know whether he's one of your followers or mine," whereupon Carson topped him with: "I don't have that loyal a following."

A splendidly hilarious specimen of Billy Graham at his rapid-fire best is his sermon on "Family and Home." In urging you to keep your house in order, he tells three stories in less than a minute. In the first, illustrating the prevalence of bickering, he tells how a burglar breaks into a home on a rainy night. He is mistaken by the lady of the house for her returning husband. "Take off your shoes!" she barks from the next room. The burglar flees, meekly and empty-handedly, because "it's like robbing my own home."

Graham's second story begins with a plea to "tell your wife you love her. But do it gently at this late date or she may faint." He tells of a husband who—for once!—remembers his wife's birthday. He comes from work with a bouquet of flowers and serenades her with *Happy Birthday to You*. She bursts into tears: "The children cried all day! The sink was stopped up! The telephone never stopped ringing! And now YOU come home drunk!"

Billy Graham goes on: "In the best-arranged home, the husband is the head. Two newlyweds had an argument about this one night. He grabbed a pair of trousers off a chair and waved them at her, saying: 'In this family, I wear these!' And she said: 'Those pants are mine!'"

There is a Bill Adler anthology called *Wit and Wisdom of Billy Graham* and there is a Bartlett-like volume, compiled and edited by Cort R. Flint, called *The Quotable Billy Graham*. But the essence of Billy Graham's preaching is a deeper mixture of joy and pain than those superficial titles imply.

"If God loves the world," he asks rhetorically, "then why the war in Vietnam? Why the hungry people in India?

There is suffering in every generation. Every generation dies. We're all born with a disease and it eventually causes death. And so the whole human race is under a sentence of death. Every generation dies.''

Here Billy Graham points an accusing finger, like Uncle Sam on the recruiting posters.

"God—loves—YOU! He sees your lonely moments. He *knows* that sin you think you can't give up. GOD ALWAYS ALWAYS ALWAYS ALWAYS LOVES—He LOVES you! And he wants to come into your heart and give you a supernatural power.''

Now Billy Graham holds the Good Book aloft.

"You want to bring peace to this world? Study this book!

"You want to solve the crime problem? Study this book!

"You want to stir men up? Study this book!

"You want to get to Heaven? Study this book!''

It is where Billy Graham finds all his answers.

> "*You say you could not forgive Manasseh? Oh, but you don't know the love and grace and mercy of God! It goes beyond ours. It is everlasting. Do you know what God did? God forgave him!* . . . *If we are willing to repent, if we are willing to return unto Him, if we are willing to come to His Son who died on the cross, the Son Whom He has given, God says, 'I will not turn a deaf ear. I will forgive, I will have mercy, I will pardon.' He died on the cross for you, and God took all of your sins and put them on Him.* [Here, with his hands, Graham makes the sound of pounding nails.] *The angels were coming to rescue Him, but He said, 'No, I want to stay on this cross so I can save them.' That's how much God loves you. Christ did all the work for your salvation. You don't have to do anything for it. All you have to do is receive it* . . .
>
> "*Think of it! Every little child burned by Manasseh, every man he had murdered, every lie he had told, every immoral thing he had done, was wiped out as though he had never committed them. In fact, the Bible goes so far as to say that God remembers our sins no more. In other words, God has the ability to forget.*
>
> "*And that wasn't the end of it. Do you know what*

God did? God took Manasseh out of that dungeon, returned him 1,500 miles back to Jerusalem, restored him to his throne, and again he was King of Judah. What joy! And that wasn't the end. The rest of his life Manasseh did all in his power to live up to the decision he had made for God in a dungeon."

Billy Graham preaches instant redemption. The only prerequisite is commitment to Christ. You have been reading plenty about Christ in these pages. Here is what Billy Graham says about commitment:

"Now you may not like the politics of Castro or Ho Chi Minh. But at least you know where they stand. Castro can spend hours telling you exactly what he thinks. I like Harry Truman for taking sides. I liked Sir Winston Churchill for taking sides. Khrushchev took sides.

"What about you? Have *you* made a decision for Christ? If you don't make a decision, He accepts it as a decision of no." Then Graham tells of a football player who intercepted a pass: "He was very sincere. But he ran the wrong way. And he lost the game."

Then he tells of a man who hit a home run and was called *out* by the umpire: "He had failed to touch first base. What about you? You go to church. You believe in God. You read the Bible. You call yourself a Christian. But you fail to touch first base! You fail to experience Christ!"

It is his simplistic preaching of instant redemption that seems to offend Billy Graham's egghead critics. Reinhold Niebuhr has complained that Graham "reduces faith to a simple panacea for all the ills of the world" and "solves all problems of life by asking bad people to become good and to prove it by loving one another." Dr. Niebuhr has been quoted in *Life* as saying that "this new evangelism promises a new life, not through painful religious experience but merely by signing a decision card."

Reviewing *World Aflame* in *Book Week,* Martin E. Marty wrote that Graham is "a humane, generous, outgoing person. But his virtues are seldom patent . . . because of the stridency of his sermons, his scoldings, his slogans. . . In the end, his message is unconvincing. . . Graham, at home in the White House and the jet set, the World's Fair and the ladies' magazines, is an implausible doom-sayer. . . We may buy *World Aflame* and enjoy it or dismiss it and go back to daily living unchanged by it."

The Billy Graham Evangelistic Association chooses to ignore many of these criticisms on the grounds that "Billy feels that, if you try to run down rumors and answer critics, you'll spend all your time defending yourself." As one high official put it: "Wasn't it Nehemiah in the Old Testament who said, 'I'm building a wall. I cannot come down and fight with my enemies.'?" Nevertheless, Niebuhr's nettles have elicited rejoinders. In his authorized biography of Graham, John Pollock writes that Niebuhr's criticism in *Life* "must have sounded odd to the increasing thousands who signed cards in token of costly decision, and completed the Bible courses or came to the regular studies for converts, and were finding their way through the adjustments inevitable in a life which had turned from self to Christ."

In 1963, Graham declared: "When Dr. Niebuhr makes his criticisms of me, I study them for I have great respect for him. I think he has helped me to apply Christianity to the social problems we face, and has helped me to comprehend what those problems are. But I disagree with Dr. Niebuhr in one respect. I don't think you can change the world, with all its lust and hate and greed, until you change men's hearts. Men must love God before they can truly love their neighbors. The theologians don't seem to understand that fact."

(Graham has stayed true to this view—even in the uproar enveloping the Kennedy assassination and its opinionated historian, William Manchester. In 1967, discussing Manchester's assertion that Dallas was "a diseased city," Graham asserted: "Nothing could be farther from the truth. Would you call Washington a diseased city because Abraham Lincoln happened to be killed there? Would you call Buffalo a diseased city because William McKinley was shot there? Would you call Miami a diseased city because Franlin Roosevelt was almost killed there?")

Preaching up Niebuhr's way—at Riverside Church near

Columbia University—in 1967, Graham disclaimed his own theological authority: *"I am not an expert on anything— except one thing: My own personal relationship to God."*

He has kept it as simple as that—ever since 1950, when that theologian named Chuck Templeton heckled him about the Bible. Billy Graham portrays a Jesus who was as thirsty as you and I would be in a desert, who ate at a table as you and I do, and who bled as you and I would.

Once, Graham was asked: "Does anybody know God?"

"Well, sir," he replied, "I don't want to sound egotistical and presumptuous—because I'd have to say it in all humility: I believe I know God. And I believe that there are tens of millions of people throughout the world today that know God as their own. They are certain that He lives in their heart.

"It's very interesting to me that the Bible never once tries to prove the existence of God. All the writers of the Scriptures assume that God exists. The Bible begins: 'In the beginning, God.' It's intuitive to believe in God. We've never found a tribe or society anywhere in the world that didn't have some sort of religion. It may be primitive and crude, but they believe in God. . .

"And I believe, as a Christian, that God was totally and completely and fully revealed in the person of Jesus Christ. And, when I want to see God, I look at Jesus Christ, because I believe that He was God incarnate."

On another occasion, Graham was asked: "Can man still talk about a *personal God* as he comes to realize how vast the universe is?"

"The vastness is only what the Bible has always described and what David sang about. We're just learning what's been there all the time, and God becomes even more personal in light of all this. It seems to me the more we know, the more insignificant we feel. Apart from God, we are nothing. This makes the fact that He would love me more wonderful."

One day, Billy Graham and his son Ned were walking down a road when they accidentally stepped on an anthill. Ned was distressed by the death and destruction they had caused.

His father told him: "Son, we've killed a lot of ants,

we've wounded a lot of them, and wrecked their home. It would be wonderful if you and I could go down there and help them rebuild and tell them that we really love them and want to help them."

"It sure would," said Ned.

"Well, you'd have to become an ant to do that," Graham said. "And there's no way to reduce yourself to their size or speak their language."

Graham tells this story often and reminds his listeners that "this was God's situation until He became a man in Jesus Christ—to help! And Jesus Christ took our sins on Him."

Before delivering his invitation, Billy Graham sometimes softens his thunder momentarily with:

"Many of you are religious. I'm not calling you to religion. I'm not calling you to Christianity. I'm calling you to the person of Jesus Christ.

"When we went to Vietnam, we had to have inoculations for various diseases. You have to take cholera and every time I take cholera I get sick. An hour after my cholera inoculation, I went to bed. I had headaches. I had fever. I had a miserable time. I had a little case of cholera—just enough to keep me from getting cholera when I went to Vietnam.

"Almost everybody in this audience has a little religion. And you're the hardest person to reach just because you've been inoculated. *You've had just enough to keep you from having the true experience of Christ.*"

Graham is fond of pointing out that "the Bible says, 'The Devil believes.' *Why, the Devil is a fundamentalist and he is orthodox!* He believes in Christ. He believes in the Bible. He believes the whole business of religion. He is even in the religion business. Intellectually, he believes in the dogma, he believes in the creed. But the Devil has never been saved and he is not going to Heaven. . . There must be a complete surrender to Christ!"

Every now and then, Billy Graham indulges in out-and-out fundamentalist moralizing:

"The Bible teaches that the life of the flesh is in the blood.

Blood represents life. But blood also represents death. You take the blood out of the arteries of a person and he'll die. Do you know that doctors used to bleed people?

"George Washington, the first President of the United States, was sick and the doctors took his blood. They did it five or six times. He got weaker and weaker. They took more blood. They thought they would save him.

"*George Washington was actually killed by his doctors*— through ignorance. But, if George Washington's doctors had read the Bible, they'd have learned that the life of the flesh is in the blood."

Billy Graham may have homogenized his message over the years, but he has not diluted it. Call it fundamentalism, liberalism, overt Southern Baptism, or latent Presbyterianism, if you will—it is all of these and none of these. Graham is a product of old-time religion, but, for most of the past two decades, he has been re-making it. In many parts of the Bible Belt today, you will find sermons and songleaders and the trappings of church services adjusting to the Billy Graham/Cliff Barrows pattern.

Graham is a living ecumenical movement. He doesn't promote or demote one institution, one denomination, or one point of view vs. another. He concentrates on inspiration. He is there on the platform to send people back to whatever religious ideal inspires them. Thus, shortly before 6 A.M. at the Easter sunrise service in San Juan, a Catholic priest appeared in the pulpit at Bithorn Stadium for a few words preceding Billy Graham's message. "We want to make it very clear," he said in Spanish, "that this meeting has the support of *all* the churches here—inside and outside the [Protestant] Evangelical Council. We have helped in one way or another to pray for this meeting."

Billy Graham preaches what he believes—and believes what he preaches. That Easter morning, he told the worshippers: "About five years ago, I put my own father in the grave. But I didn't say goodbye, I said I'll see you soon. I will see him in Heaven. We will be reunited. There will be a glorious day in Heaven."

Billy Graham doesn't feel like jumping into his iced tea

when you question him about this. He believes. And he walks with a spring in his step *because* he believes.

> *"I want to tell you tonight that God can do for you what He did for Manasseh. God says that he will not only forgive you because of Christ, but also because of Christ He will restore you to the position that you occupied before Adam sinned. He'll do more than that! He'll make you a joint heir with His Son Jesus Christ, and some day you shall rule and reign with Him. He'll give you peace and joy in the midst of a troubled world of turmoil down here. You will be able to meet your problems and difficulties and sufferings in life with a new peace and a new dynamic power that you have never known. The Bible says He admits you into His family and you become a child of God, a member of the royal family of Heaven with royal blood in your veins. That's what God does. And the moment you die, your body goes to the grave— but the real you, your spirit, goes to be with Him FOREVER!*
>
> *"Ladies and gentlemen—that is what God offers you tonight—free! You don't have to pay for it. What is your sin? He can forgive you. He can come into your heart. He can give you a new life. Are you an intellectual? Are you a student? Or a professor at the university? I've seen many professors come to the cross. Do you know how they come? Like a little child—by simple faith. Why? Because you cannot come to God by intellect alone! Our intellect will not lead us to God. Our intellect has been blinded by sin."*

One morning Billy Graham alluded to a 1966 work of mine that I wouldn't have dreamed of sending him:

"I've quoted your *Life* article on topless waitresses several times in my sermon on 'Moral Alternatives.' * It gave me the opportunity to describe a situation in America that I couldn't very well go to see for myself."

Try to imagine Billy Graham skewering Chinese tid-

---

* In this sermon, usually given to groups of businessmen or students, Graham sketches the choice between total license and total control before proposing a third solution—the ''moral and spiritual economics'' of a religious reawakening.

bits at San Francisco's Topless-a-Gong-Gong, and you can comprehend his research problem. Not necessarily through choice, Billy Graham has to be just about the most detached of all intellectuals. His life has confined him to the ivory tower of setting an example. There are very few entertainments he can attend without his presence either implying endorsement or obscuring the event itself.

I remarked that curling up with a good novel was probably his best bet for cultural recreation.

"I don't read any books for pleasure. I never read novels," he replied categorically. "My reading for pleasure is limited to *The New York Times* Book Review and *The* [London] *Times* Literary Supplement. I read about the novels in their reviews. There's so much more to be read in the Bible."

"Do you mean to say," I asked the man I'd already pronounced an intellectual, "that you've never read a novel?"

"Not recently," he said, *"Dr. Zhivago* was the last novel I read. I struggled through that one and then had to go to the movie to find out what it was about. Before that, I read *Exodus*. Actually, I probably average one novel a year, but only because my wife pushes me to it."

"Was *Dr. Zhivago* the last movie you saw?"

"No. I saw *The Bible* and I was delighted with it. The thing I liked that John Huston did was his keeping to the story of the Bible—his acceptance of the miracles of the Bible. When I saw the story of Abraham and Isaac on the screen, I came out of the theater with a sense of dedication.

"I average one or two movies a year. I'm offered private screenings, but I only accept the ones that really interest me. Mr. de Mille and Walter Disney were friends of mine. Charlton Heston and Mr. de Mille once presented me with the Ten Commandments carved in stone.

"In my talks, I allude to more movies than I see, because here too I depend upon reviews. I have discussed certain movies like *The Silence* and certain Broadway plays, but I get much of my material from listening to Judith Crist on the 'Today' show. I have never seen a Broadway play—I take that back, I saw one, *Oklahoma!* And in London I saw *My Fair Lady*. I would have been very interested in seeing

Graham talks with hands as well as heart and mouth.

that play about the Incas [*Royal Hunt of the Sun*], but I missed it."

His allusion to Ingmar Bergman's *The Silence*—a Swedish film best remembered for its lesbianism, nihilism, and public urination—prompted me to ask Graham if he had seen it.

"I don't think I could ever attend it," he replied, "simply because of what it's about. I feel that some of these realistic movies are playing on the emotions of the spectators and I don't think I ought to set an example by going to such things. Bishop Pike once gave a controversial picture —I forget which one—a great deal of publicity when his photo was taken in front of it. If I want realism, I can read the first chapter of Romans."

For the record, *The Silence* was, if anything, *surrealistic*. After a cryptic train journey, it was set in a deserted hotel in a lifeless city. I held my tongue, however, while Graham continued in this vein:

"I disapprove of these movies. They are made to make money and perhaps they succeed. But *My Fair Lady* and *The Sound of Music* and Mr. Disney's films have been overwhelming successes because they're clean and wholesome. I felt the same way about *Who's Afraid of Virginia Woolf?* that I did about *The Silence*. I read the reviews. I don't need to see it. I know its message, if any. I'm reasonably certain I would have come away feeling nothing but depressed . . .

"I'm not afraid of the temptation. I see enough that's sordid on television without going to a theater for it. It's a waste of time to be left feeling nothing except that I want to take a bath."

Billy Graham has a sense of mission, a sense of humor, a sense of style, and remarkable sensitivity to other people. What I detected here and on perhaps one other occasion, was a deficiency in artistic sensibility. Kathryn Abbe, whose photos are the principal illustrations for this report, wanted a picture of Graham golfing—but this was a day when he wasn't. He told her so, but added helpfully that the BGEA staff photographer, Russ Busby, had taken some golf shots a day earlier. He would be glad to give them to her and, if she wished, she could say she'd taken them.

Mrs. Abbe shook her head so vehemently that her sun-hat almost flopped off.

Later, when just Graham and I were walking on the beach, Graham volunteered that he hoped he hadn't "hurt Mrs. Abbe's feelings."

Billy Graham has acted guardedly in the presence of photographers ever since 1950, when the Atlanta *Constitution* embarrassed him with its depiction of the money-bags from the "love offering." The following year, he stopped in Hawaii on his way to Korea. "At the airport, two girls in grass skirts greeted me and kissed me on each cheek. And the photographers took pictures. Well, I began to think about this—and, remember, this was a time before the jets, so not everybody knew that this happened to everybody who arrived in Hawaii—and the more I thought about it, the more I worried. The photo had already gone out on the Associated Press wire, but we were able to intercept it before it got past San Francisco. The bureau chief there agreed to kill the picture."

In 1956 in Louisville, a woman photographer had to wait in a special office at the Brown Hotel, rather than in the Graham suite. "Only recently," an aide explained to her, "Mr. Graham went for a ride with his sister and people called us to ask what our evangelist was doing out with a blonde."

A few years ago, Graham was passing through the airport in a city that was about to be blessed with a Playboy Club. "All of a sudden," Graham recalls, "a girl came up to me, took off her coat, and there she was in a bunny outfit. Grady Wilson jumped in between us just as the flash bulbs went off. Then I made a fast getaway.

"In London last year, I was riding a minicar in a motorcade through Soho. There were crowds all around us and we were hardly moving when I noticed a girl being passed over the top of the crowd—on people's shoulders and over their heads. She was unzipping as she went. When I saw this, I simply said, 'God bless you. Good night', and got out of the car and disappeared into the crowd of policemen.

She was a stripper and when the people who'd put her up to this got her on top of my car, she had nothing on."

The moral may be that if Billy Graham will not go to the topless, the topless will come to him. In any event, the pressure of potential scandal is so great (an East Berlin newspaper once had him dating "a blonde named Beverly Shea") that his image-watching sometimes verges on shadow-boxing. I was not surprised when Graham declined to let Kathryn Abbe photograph him in a bathing suit. But I was startled by the language of diplomacy he used in saying no:

"A photographer once took a picture of me in a bathing suit and I said to him: 'Would you take a picture of Pope Paul—not that I put myself in that category—or Bishop Fulton J. Sheen in a bathing suit?' "

Still, far more sophisticated men have achieved a tiny fraction of Billy Graham's renown and, within six months, decomposed into caricatures of themselves. It is to Billy Graham's credit that he remains flesh-and-blood after nearly two decades in the limelight. He can scarcely be faulted, at this late date, for starting to blur a little around the edges.

"If you want to have the joy and peace of the new life, you must receive Christ in your heart. First, you must repent of your sins. You must say, like Manasseh, 'Forgive me, O Lord!' Secondly, you must receive Christ into your heart by simple childlike faith. And the third thing that you must do: You must confess Him openly as your Saviour. That's the reason I ask you to come forward. I don't ask you to come forward because I want to see you walk across the grass. I call you because it's important Biblically and psychologically. Every person that Christ called in the New Testament He called publicly. Jesus said: 'If you're not willing to acknowledge Me before men, I'll not acknowledge you before My Father Which art in Heaven.' There's something about coming forward and standing here quietly that settles it in your own life."

Here begins the invitation. At the organ, Don Hustad will

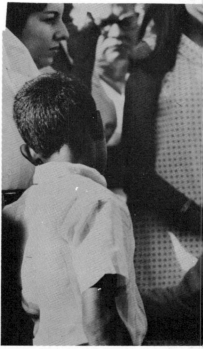
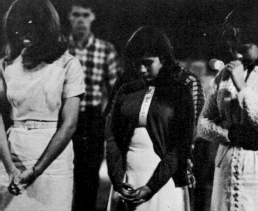

"You must confess Him openly as your Saviour. Every person that Christ called in the New Testament He called publicly. There's something about coming forward that settles it in your own life."

play *Just As I Am* and, whenever Graham pauses to pray or meditate in silence, the choir will sing very softly behind Hustad.*

"We sort of pace it to what's happening on the podium," Hustad told me. "When he breaks in to say a word, the choir stops and the organ continues. If he wants to give people more time to come forward, he'll say 'I want us to sing another hymn' and we'll do *Almost Persuaded*. For the past 15 years, those are the only two songs he's used for this purpose."

They are the same two songs the choir sang in Charlotte in 1934 when Billy Graham came forward after Mordecai Ham had preached.

Several times in his career, Billy Graham has refuted critics who claimed it was the music, not the message, that brought converts forward. (This theory holds that the organ music accompanying the invitation is played so softly that you have to *lean* forward to hear it, which puts you in a posture conducive to *going* forward.) Stung by this analysis, Graham has then conducted his next service without *any* music. There have been as many converts as the night before—often more.

One London critic then complained about "Graham's use of long, meaningful, dramatic silence."

> *"Give yourself to Christ tonight. Let Him forgive your sins. Let Him come into your heart and change your life. I'm going to ask you to get up out of your seats, hundreds of you—from the balconies, in the television rooms, all over this place. Get out of your seats and come and stand in front of this platform and say by coming: 'I'm willing to give up my sins. I'm willing to receive Christ as my Saviour.' Now if you're with friends or relatives or you've come in a group, they'll wait. But you come. If you have a friend with you, you can bring your friend with you. But come. Just get up out of your seat and stand here."*

---

* Don Hustad left the Team in September, 1967, to become Professor of Church Music at Southern Baptist Seminary in Louisville.

116

"They come. Always they come," Billy Graham marveled once. "Always the sight moves me and fills me again with wonderment at the power of the Gospel. I give the invitation to come forward, to get up in the crowd, to say inwardly and yet to all the world, 'I am publicly committing my life to Christ as Lord and Saviour.' As we await their response, I feel an almost childlike sense of expectancy. And when they begin to stir and rise—one here, one there, and finally sometimes thousands—I know again that I am a mere spectator watching a miracle in which my part was very small."

At such a miracle at Wembley—when more than 2,000 made decisions for Christ in one day—the Archbishop of Canterbury remarked to associate evangelist Grady Wilson: "We'll never see a sight like that again until we get to Heaven."

Grady Wilson put his arm around the Primate of all England and said: "That's right, Brother Archbishop."

The response to Billy Graham's invitation is indeed a wondrous spectacle. You may always remember the creak of footfalls on wooden boards in London or the rain of *señoritas'* stiletto heels on concrete in Puerto Rico. In particular I will never forget the sight—night after night—of an illuminated baseball diamond coming alive with the glow of people.

First, a couple of lone individuals or a husband and wife or two sons and their mother advance with grave dignity toward second base—above where Billy Graham stands, Bible in hand, praying them forward.

Then come clusters of people: whole families hand-in-hand. . . working men in T-shirts; businessmen with brief cases . . . women with mantillas and umbrellas; men with newspapers and Bibles . . . tourists in Madras jackets and Satan-red Bermuda shorts . . . fathers and mothers cradling sleeping babes-in-arms . . . four generations of one family (the third generation notably pregnant) . . . little girls wearing white pumps and little boys wearing polka-dotted bowties . . . a skinny girl, her long arm so entwined around the hammy bicep of a fat girl that it's hard to tell whether she's propelling or restraining her.

Mostly, these are "ordinary folk," but their many splendored hues of hair and skin and clothing make the diamond radiant with color.

One of BGEA's many surveys of its converts indicates that, if a thousand people came forward one night, 460 of them would have no church affiliation at all. The rest would range from lip-service church members to devout church-goers "re-dedicating" their lives to Christ.

Taking the same thousand occupationally—from a survey of 14,000 of them—an average of two would be from the "intellectual professions" like doctoring and college professing; two would be wealthy owners of large businesses; one would be a law-enforcement officer, 15 school-teachers; at least 110 sales or office people or skilled tradesmen, at least 120 semi-skilled or industrial workers. More than half the rest would be students, housewives, military personnel, and "miscellaneous."

Some of those who come forward attract special notice: a dozen deaf mutes and their interpreter (they are intercepted by a counselor who greets them in sign language) . . . choir members descending from Billy Graham's platform to join the ranks of converts . . . ushers and policemen who become part of the event they are here to control . . . a handful of teenagers wearing boots, Iron Crosses, and swastikas on their black-leather jackets. A couple of Crusade aides and several counselors move in quietly behind them in case they are here to make trouble. But they gawk at Billy Graham for a few minutes and then go away. BGEA is aware that some of those who come forward do so only to be seen or to win bets or to get closer looks at the star of the show they've come to see. The "inquiry" statistics that are given out after each Crusade meeting, however, are confined strictly to those who have been interviewed and processed by counselors.

Some come running. Four young men, who made a late start from the farthest reaches of the stadium, arrive like a relay team—out-of-breath but urging each other forward. Children in Superman capes and Batman masks romp in and out of the quiet, solemn throng before second base.

Some who started early are among the last to arrive: a teen-age boy tapping the white cane of the nearly blind . . . a paraplegic hobbling on two canes . . . an old woman with a son and two grandsons helping her forward. Every night in San Juan, I saw the same middle-aged invalid wearing bathrobe and pajamas, being pushed forward in a wheelchair by his wife.

> *"You may not be a member of any church. You may be Catholic, Protestant, or Jewish. I don't know who you are. But you WANT Jesus Christ as your Lord and your Master and your Saviour and you want YOUR sins forgiven. . . . I'm going to ask you to come—as hundreds have already done. Whatever your past; whoever you are; social standing; education—you come. We're going to wait.*
>
> *"From up in the stands—you have to get up and go down the stairs. It takes three or four minutes to come. So start right now from everywhere. There's a little voice down inside that has spoken to you. That's the spirit of God. Don't you harden your heart. Don't you put it off. You come now, while you can.*
>
> *"Young man, young woman, father, mother, whoever you may be. You just come now. We're going to wait.*
>
> *"You may be a choir member who's been here all this time and God has spoken to you. You need Christ. You may be an usher here. But God has spoken to you and you want to come.*
>
> *"We're going to wait on you. There's plenty of time and I'm going to ask that nobody leave this stadium, please. Just everyone quietly praying as people get up out of their seats from everywhere and come. That's it—quickly! Just come on now."*

Why do people come forward? Whole books have been written seeking without success to explain the upturned faces before the pulpit. Curtis Mitchell's *Those Who Came Forward* quotes a Chicago housewife: "I hung onto my seat with might and main, but I felt myself lifted and suddenly I was out in the aisle and walking forward on feet that seemed to wear wings.'' Mitchell also quotes a California divorcee who makes it sound sensual: ''I knew on the instant that my surrender was complete and I couldn't get to the front fast enough. I was cleansed and full of joy for the first time in years.'' Amidst hundreds of other interviews and case histories, Mitchell seeks to analyze the invisible tugging that Christians call ''God's leading.''

Billy Graham's gift of the invitation is one of those phenomena, like Richard Nixon's 5 o'clock-shadow and the Kennedy mystique, that mass communications have made intensely personal. But, even the first time she overheard him in 1940, Ruth Bell sensed that ''you weren't impressed by his earnestness, you weren't impressed by his gestures, you were impressed that there was Someone speaking to you besides Bill. There was another voice than his.''

Graham's authorized biographer, John Pollock, states:

''The charge is sometimes made against the Crusades that though Billy Graham is personally sincere he puts across what is virtually an immense confidence trick, by the manipulation of crowds, the singing and the lights to produce decisions in a whirl of emotion and a mental vacuum. This charge breaks down against the fact that similar results follow his university preaching and discussions.

''Graham is essentially a preacher to the individual, whether in a crowd of one or twenty, of a hundred or a hundred thousand. He is vividly aware of the dangers of mass psychosis. He never preaches to evoke a crowd response, but selects in his mind one unknown member of the audience and aims to reach the whole of that man—his intellect, his conscience, and his will.''

> *"You may be a crippled person. You may be an ill person. You may be a bereaved person. But Christ conquered that problem for you. You can rise above it with His help. Give your life to Him tonight. Surrender your heart and say: 'From tonight on, by God's grace, I'm going to make my decision and commitment for Him. Tonight I'm going to start leading a new life. And, from tonight on, I'm going to start reading my Bible and*

praying and growing. I want to be a clean wholesome Christian. I want to turn from my sins. I want to receive Christ. I want to be CONVERTED!' The word CONVERTED means 'to be changed around.' Will you say that tonight? Hundreds of you? Thousands of you?"

In London two years ago, two strangers met on their way forward for Christ and one of them, a pickpocket, said to the other: "I had better give you back your wallet now!" In another episode, a 19-year-old father went straight from his counseling interview to a police station, where he confessed to 42 crimes—mostly breaking-and-entering. He received three months in a detention home.

"Come right up now while the choir sings another hymn. The decision is up to you. No one can make it for you. I remember when I sat there in that tabernacle in Charlotte, North Carolina, they were singing this song when I went forward. That first step was the hardest I ever took in my life. But when I took it God did the rest. I woke up the next morning and I KNEW I'd been changed. You can make a great decision tonight that will change your life. You can be born again. The first step is such a simple one that people stumble over it. The man with the Ph. D. must come like a little child—and that's hard for a businessman, socialite, labor leader to come."

The most impressive way to watch the spectacle of newborn and reaffirmed Christians responding to Billy Graham's invitation is from high in the stands—a trickle that becomes a stream and then a torrent and sometimes a flood. But whenever I left the press box and stood near the platform—watching them converge as Billy Graham might see it—I was reminded that many faces coming forward belonged to counselors, joining the converts to interview them later.

The Graham organizations make no effort to conceal the counselors' presence, so it must be reiterated here that their "inquiry statistics"—unlike many secular and religious crowd figures—are scrupulously honest. In fact, the statistics are given out largely to *prevent* exaggerations by news-

121

men who would count the counselors. Nonetheless, the injection of counselors at this point does lend an illusion of still vaster numbers, which might impel the wavering to join the throng.

Whenever possible, a Graham Crusade has one counselor interview one inquirer—to find out his motive for coming forward, to ascertain his specific needs, and to find an appropriate passage of Scripture to help him start his new life. Sometimes, there is a shortage of counselors or an unanticipated deluge of inquirers—in which case a counselor will interview a number of converts—turning one over to an advisor and going on to the next. (An advisor heads a platoon of counselors.) But anything less than 1-to-1 counseling is frowned upon by BGEA. Fernando Vangioni had tears in his eyes one night in Ponce when he told me of a couple of hundred inquirers going away angrily (and without leaving their names) after waiting 45 minutes to be counseled.

The counselors are grouped unobtrusively near the front of the stands during Billy Graham's sermon. During the invitation, as people begin to converge on the platform, an advisor beckons one of his counselors to follow a specific individual forward. Counselors are paired with converts primarily by sex and age, but also (whenever manpower permits) by dress, mannerism, nationality, and even race. It has proved effective to have student counsel student and Negro counsel Negro; they tend to speak each other's language and understand each other's problems.

"The local ministers recommend counselors to us," said Crusades Director Walter Smyth. "We used to say, 'Send us your spiritual people,' but now we say 'send everybody' —because, whether or not they work out as counselors, the training is invaluable to them."

When I was in Atlanta, Smyth's executive assistant for Crusade planning, Forrest Layman, briefed me on the counselor training program. It started in 1950, when Billy Graham began "having sleepless nights over what happened to people after they came forward. . . . In training a counselor, we emphasize that his function is to channel the inquirer rather than to change him and that the man who is reached is more important than the method of reaching him. Our training programs are usually given once a week. Some have lasted as long as nine weeks, but five weeks are customary for covering the material without wearying the student before he ever goes to work as a counselor.''

In Los Angeles in 1963, there were 23,800 enrolled in counselor-training classes. In London in 1966, there were 30,000 who began and 6,000 who finished.

Layman gave me a lesson outline. The first week's training covers "Basic Qualifications of a Counselor" ("must know Christ as personal Saviour . . . living and abiding in Christ . . . practical working knowledge of the Scriptures . . . a willing heart . . ." etc.). The second week covers "Counseling for Restoration"—that is, for Christians who come forward to "recommit, rededicate, or reconsecrate" themselves ("Eternal vigilance is the price of liberty"). Third week: "Counseling the [Hitherto] Unconverted" ("Conversion defined: *The new birth is the giving of God's own nature to the one who is born anew.* . . . Conversion brought about: . . . *God said it is His Word, Christ did it on the cross, I believe it in my heart, and that settles it!*") Fourth week: "New Testament Principles of Follow-Up (how Christ did it; how Paul did it.)"

After the fourth week, the student must apply in written form to become a counselor. If he is accepted, he learns in the fifth week "the actual mechanics of counseling in a Crusade setting." At this time he is handed an 18-minute script of a sample interview between counselor and convert. The first two minutes follow:

COUNSELOR: "Hello, there, my name is Bob Allan."
INQUIRER: "I am Bill Jones" (they shake hands).
COUNSELOR: "What do you do for a living, Bill?"
INQUIRER: "I'm a second-year student at the university."
COUNSELOR: "What are you studying there?"
INQUIRER: "Well, I'm changing my program over now from psychology to anthropology."
COUNSELOR: "Very interesting fields, I'm sure. I'm in

the insurance business myself. But you know, Bill, regardless of what kind of business we're in, an even more important thing to us is our relationship to God, and as your counselor tonight I would like very briefly to help you understand what your relationship is to God.''

INQUIRER: "I would like that very much.''

COUNSELOR: "Can you tell me why you came forward tonight, Bill?"

INQUIRER: "Well, it's a bit difficult to put in words. It seems that as Mr. Graham was preaching he was speaking right to me and when he said come forward if you want help, there was nothing else for me to do than to come forward. So here I am.''

COUNSELOR: "Fine. This is the same experience that many people have who attend this kind of Crusade meeting. In fact, it was my experience in a similar Crusade about six years ago. Let's take a few minutes to see from God's Word what He says about your spiritual needs. (*Counselor opens Bible to Romans 3:23*) * Would you like to read this verse aloud to me, please?"

It is hammered home at all five lectures that the counselor's personality should never be obtrusive: "The counselor should be the forgotten man in the experience of conversion.''

If a convert raises some thorny question, either personal or theological, that a counselor cannot handle, the latter is told to raise his hand and his advisor will step in.

Even if a counselor doesn't raise his hand, his advisor may notice that there is difficulty and step in himself or send in another counselor. A counselor is trained to withdraw immediately if tapped on the shoulder by his adviser.

In a dressing room, a tent, a courtyard, an office, or (at Madison Square Garden) the circus stables, the counselor fills out a card with basic biographical details on the inquirer plus some motivational research (check one: ☐ Acceptance of Christ as Saviour and Lord ☐ Rededication ☐ Assurance of Salvation) and hands him a booklet called

---

* "For all have sinned, and come short of the glory of God.''

My Personal Commitment containing his first Bible Study correspondence lesson.

Within 48 hours, the counselor phones or visits the convert and files a follow-up report on him (☐Lesson No. 1 completed by inquirer ☐Lesson No. 1 mailed to office ☐John 3:16 memorized * ☐I have encouraged inquirer to start Lesson 2 ☐Have encouraged inquirer to be faithful in church attendance)

"The counselor must be sensitive to the inquirer when he pays his follow-up call," Forrest Layman told me. "If the person doesn't want to be bothered, the counselor shouldn't push it. Our other four or five segments of follow-up may prove more effective."

These "segments" are initiated on the night of conversion by a crew of volunteer typists stationed in the arena. Working into the early morning hours after the last convert and the last counselor have left the ball park, they operate according to a 180-page "Co-Labor Corps of Follow-Up Department Manual." When they are done, two follow-up letters signed by Billy Graham will go out to each convert—on the fourth and tenth day after conversion. The other "segments" of follow-up include the Bible Study correspondence course; the conscience prod when the free one-year subscription to *Decision* begins; and the pastor's follow-up.

A pastor in a convert's neighborhood is sent a follow-up form with a Business Reply card. If he doesn't respond within two weeks, he is sent a second letter. If there is no reply after two more weeks, the convert's name is referred to another pastor.

In some areas, pastor follow-up has been the weakest link in a Billy Graham Crusade. A survey of 450 converts from the Madison Square Garden meetings in 1957 showed that more than half had been ignored by the churches to which they had been referred. Less than a quarter had been visited in person by a pastor; another quarter had been contacted perfunctorily by phone or letter. Ever since then,

---

* "For God so loved the world, that He gave His only begotten Son," etc.

BGEA has shored up its contacts with aggressive churches in each community, such as Norman Vincent Peale's Marble Collegiate Church in Manhattan and Gordon Powell's St. Stephen's Presbyterian Church in Sydney. Peale has written that "our church has profited in a wonderful way" from Graham's preaching. In 1959, Powell received follow-up forms for 646 converts, of whom 404 (including six M.D.s) promptly became members of his church. Two years later, more than half were regular and active churchgoers; less than a quarter had dropped away entirely.

Do conversions last? Another of the omnipresent BGEA surveys shows that, of those making their first commitment to Christ at a Crusade, two-thirds are still in some church five years later. The most graphic testimony, however, can be found in Curtis Mitchell's *Those Who Came Forward:*

. . . From a satyric, prurient-minded London physician: "After accepting Christ I could not reconcile my old taste in literature with my new experience, and anyway my appetite had changed. One night . . . I threw my sensational literature and pinup calendars over London Bridge into the River Thames. A suspicious policeman rushed to inquire what the bundle contained and was very skeptical when I told him the truth."

. . . A California convert startled his community with the news that "from now on, my real estate office will be closed on Sundays." He told his salesmen to "go to church on Sunday and don't make any appointments for the Lord's day." They protested that "Sunday's the best business day of the week. You'll go under for sure!"—but his business thrived and soon he had to open up a branch office.

. . . From a Texas businessman: "You know, I'd had a lot of trouble with my stomach, and I don't have that kind of trouble any more. I'm not worrying all the time. . . Now you won't believe this, but it has even changed my golf. Yes sir, it has taken six strokes off my game."

"From today on, I want you to start reading your Bible. That helps you to grow. You can't grow without reading

the Scriptures and studying. We're going to give you some verses today—to memorize. Secondly, I want you to spend time every day in prayer. That's when you talk to God. And God will answer your prayer from now on. Thirdly: Witness for Christ. How do you witness? By going home tonight and being kind, tender, loving, forgiving, gracious, thoughtful, LOVING! Then people will come and say: 'Well, Jim, what's happened to you? You're different.' That's when you tell them 'Christ changed my life.' THAT'S witnessing! Then fourthly: Get into the church. Get into the church and get to work for Christ. Stay loyal and faithful to the church—the church where Christ preached. Get to work for Him!

"You say, 'There are a lot of things about the church I don't like. There are a lot of hypocrites and all the rest of them.' Many people ask me, 'Can't you be a Christian and not go to church?' That would be like being a sailor and not being in the Navy—or a soldier not assigned some regiment. NO, THE CHURCH IS NOT PERFECT! It never will be perfect on this earth! But we go into the church because it's Christ's organization on earth. And we're to love the church.

"Now I'm going to ask that we bow our heads in prayer. I want you to pray this prayer after me—out loud, PRAY IT OUT LOUD!:

"Oh God. I am a sinner. I'm sorry for my sins. I'm willing to turn from my sins. I receive Christ as Saviour. I confess Him as Lord. From this moment on, I want to serve Him and follow Him in the fellowship of His church. In Christ's name, Amen!"

Thus does Billy Graham end the meeting. Now the counselors lead the converts away to be interviewed. On your way out, the choir is reprising *How Great Thou Art* and probably you are singing, humming, or maybe even whistling it, too.

When Christ shall come with shout of acclamation
And take me home, what joy shall fill my heart!

Then I shall bow in humble adoration
And there proclaim, my God, how great Thou art!*

The song is addressed to God, not to Billy Graham, for it is here that "the man with God's message" fades swiftly out of the picture. He leaves his converts in the foreground savoring a blessing that only mother, father, spouse, or God can grant: *He accepts you just as you are.* In preaching his simple universal message, he frees you from your hang-ups and releases you to do better.

Not everybody listens. Not everybody hears Billy Graham. We march to many different drummers and the small miracle that is Billy Graham cannot always cut through the jingle-jangle-jingle of old-time evangelism or the clatter of crutches in certain churchyards.

At 7:41 on Easter morning in San Juan, the cripple who had come forward night after night in his wheelchair was waiting near the platform. It was, after all, the day of resurrection. And so, as Billy Graham came down to earth, the man stood up. He waved away his wife. He tried to take the four or five steps that would bring him to Billy Graham, not to God. And so he crumpled in a heap behind the retreating back of "God's special messenger to these crisis days." If Billy Graham had seen him fall, he certainly would have stopped to help. But when his own part in the ritual is over, his exit is as swift as mercury. He looks neither right nor left nor back, for the rest is in Christ's hands and Billy Graham is now virtually invisible. He dons a white raincoat and, in three giant strides, he boards a white Ford that whisks him away to the nearest Holiday Inn without so much as a "God bless you real good."

THE END